A LIGHT ON PEACHTREE

A LIGHT ON PEACHTREE

A History of the Atlanta Woman's Club

written by

Anne B. Jones

with photographs by

Aryc W. Mosher

Mercer University Press

Macon, Georgia

MERCER
UNIVERSITY PRESS

Endowed by
TOM WATSON BROWN
and
THE WATSON-BROWN FOUNDATION, INC.

MUP/ H838

© 2012 Mercer University Press
1400 Coleman Avenue
Macon, Georgia 31207

First Edition

Books published by Mercer University Press are printed on
acid-free paper that meets the requirements of American National
Standard for Information Sciences—Permanence of Paper
for Printed Library Materials.

Mercer University Press is a member of Green Press Initiative
(greenpressinitiative.org), a nonprofit organization working to help
publishers and printers increase their use of recycled paper and
decrease their use of fiber derived from endangered forests.
This book is printed on recycled paper.

ISBN   978-0-88146-275-3

*Cataloging-in-Publication Data is available
from the Library of Congress*

Text design by Burt&Burt
Text typeset in Warnock Pro, Chaparral Pro, Perpetua Titling

A Light on Peachtree:
A History of the Atlanta Woman's Club
is dedicated to the members
of the Atlanta Woman's Club, past and present,
who have truly been women of power, action, and light.

ACKNOWLEDGEMENTS

by Anne B. Jones

he members of the Atlanta Woman's Club wish to acknowledge other clubs of the Georgia Federation of Women's Clubs, the General Federation of Women's Clubs, and all of the men, women, clubs, organizations, and agencies who have valiantly worked for the good of our community, state, and country. Without their joint efforts, much progress and many achievements would never have been possible. The Atlanta Woman's Club's accomplishments are many, but members rarely act alone.

Every reasonable effort has been made to obtain accurate and comprehensive information for this chronicle. In a work spanning well over a century and encompassing a proliferation of historical material, not everything can be included. Because the work contains memories, opinions, sometimes unclear sequences, and anecdotes, questions on minor details may well remain. We have been careful to present this work as factually as possible. It is our fervent hope that this book will inspire other clubs to write their own histories, as so much has been accomplished by so many.

Much of our research material has been obtained from the General Federation of Women's Clubs headquarters in Washington, DC, the Atlanta History Center, the Georgia Archives, the Athens Woman's Club, and historical records maintained in the Wimbish House. In many cases, references are incomplete, often lacking dates, names, and official titles. Examples of tremendous efforts of sustained support include community endeavors such as contributions, scholarships, campaigns, and volunteer work related to all aspects of Atlanta's arts, civic affairs, and humanitarian efforts.

Much appreciation goes to former Atlanta Woman's Club president Dr. Karen M. Thomson, who proposed the writing and title of *A Light on Peachtree: A History of the Atlanta Woman's Club*, and to her husband Tom. Both helped in the research as did other club members. Many thanks are due photographer Aryc Mosher. Among those providing resource material, interviews, and other support were Daisy Luckey Aukerman, Sarah Helen Killgore, Louise Vernon, Judine Heard, Karen Clydesdale, Lisa

Banes, Karen Bacheller, and Lucy Willard as well as many other members of the Club. The staff of the Kenan Research Center of the Atlanta History Center also gave great assistance, as well as non-member volunteers Brenda Bozeman, Jo Harris Brenner, A. Louise Staman, Judy Martin, Cheryl Hilderbrand, George B. Mettler, Doyle Renolds, Kelli Perkins, Patsy Vedder Clark, and Rita Fallamal. Dinah Peevy of Tallulah Falls School, and Rose Ditto, former president of the General Federation of Women's Clubs, also deserve recognition for their contributions. We extend special gratitude to President and Mrs. Jimmy Carter for their efforts and support in writing the Foreword.

PROLOGUE

by Anne B. Jones

rom boardrooms to ballrooms, the Atlanta Woman's Club has exerted its influence in steering the development and identity of Atlanta since 1895. Headquartered in the lavishly designed and historical Wimbish House on Peachtree Street, the elegance of the Club's members contrasts sharply with their capacity for work. Through their affiliation with the Georgia and General Federation of Women's Clubs, members have helped improve the quality of life in Atlanta, the South and the world in the fields of politics, human rights, poverty, the arts, education, health, conservation and the understanding of international affairs.

As educational advocates, members worked to set the foundation of the Atlanta public kindergarten system and Georgia's public library system. In addition, along with other Georgia Federation of Women's Club members, the Atlanta Woman's Club has had a monumental effect on the development of Tallulah Falls School, one of the top-rated preparatory schools in the country, which draws students from all over the world. They also helped establish the first farmers' market in metro Atlanta, and they were instrumental in promoting the acquisition of a landing field and the building of what is now Hartsfield-Jackson Atlanta International Airport.

Few are aware of the Club's enormous effect on its community and state, or its ties to the Georgia Federation of Women's Clubs (GaFWC) and the General Federation of Women's Clubs (GFWC), both of which have been a major force in our state's and nation's history. *A Light on Peachtree: A History of the Atlanta Woman's Club* is the story of the Atlanta Woman's Club's struggles and triumphs, and the remarkable efforts and accomplishments of its members from 1895 to the present time.

—Anne B. Jones, Ph.D.

he Atlanta Woman's Club is a nonprofit, nonpartisan, nonsectarian organization begun in 1895 by resolute women to serve their community, country, and world by generously giving of their time and resources. Driving their dedication was a desire to ameliorate suffering, poverty, injustice, and poor health. Rosalynn and I are pleased to note that the AWC goals are similar to the principles by which our own nonprofit organization was started twenty-eight years ago. The Carter Center, in partnership with Emory University, is guided by a commitment to human rights and the alleviation of human suffering. Further, it seeks to prevent and resolve conflicts, enhance freedom and democracy, and improve health. When we were asked to write the foreword for *A Light on Peachtree: A History of the Atlanta Woman's Club*, we were honored and excited to participate and recognized the value of this book in enhancing awareness of the Atlanta Woman's Club and pride in the outstanding contributions it has made in helping to make Atlanta the successful world-class city it is today.

Many in Atlanta may not realize that our city and the state of Georgia could have faced a very different history had it not been for the successful advocacy and funding of several important projects undertaken by the Atlanta Woman's Club, most notably with the inception and development of the Atlanta airport. In a meeting initiated by the AWC president in 1925 with the mayor, the Club's president, Mrs. Norman Sharp, urged the purchase of a "landing field" south of Atlanta. As a result, the mayor appointed her as a member of the City Landing Field Committee, and she later was elected First Vice President of the Atlanta Chapter of the National Aeronautical Association from which the Atlanta airport evolved. It wasn't long before all of the states in the South were seeking a way to capitalize on the increasing use of aviation as a principal means to transport people and goods throughout America. Atlanta was first in getting a foothold as a connected city, which allowed us to pull ahead of other large communities. The presence of the "busiest airport in the world," the Atlanta Hartsfield-Jackson International Airport as it has come to be known now nearly ninety years after that initial meeting, has enabled our vibrant city to

XII   A LIGHT ON PEACHTREE

attract and keep job-generating businesses like Delta Airlines and Home Depot, while also preserving our lifelong relationship with Coca-Cola. How fortunate that Atlanta was able to take this geographic and economic lead, and for the impetus of the Atlanta Woman's Club.

The Atlanta Woman's Club has a long history of improving the artistic, social, and economic atmosphere of the greater Atlanta area. These hardworking, intelligent, dedicated women enriched Atlanta's cultural life by having the city's first art gallery, a library of thousands of books, and a technologically advanced auditorium that has been the setting for numerous performances including operas, concerts, and recitals from the 1920s until the 1980s—all located in the Wimbish House, the "home of the Atlanta Woman's Club" located at Peachtree and 14th Street. The women also founded the "Sweet Auburn Curb Market" to help farmers sell their produce to Atlanta residents, and it still thrives today.

Always concerned for women and children, the AWC supported early efforts to end the exploitation of minors through its support of child labor laws, compulsory education, the incorporation of kindergartens into the public school system, and educational opportunities for rural children. Also, in cooperation with the Southern Railway Company, the AWC established a mobile lending library that reached rural areas. These club members, so desirous of helping and empowering others, developed a co-op exchange program, which created the opportunity for women in rural areas to sell their crafts, despite working at home in order to raise their children.

Even the Carter Center has benefited from this generosity. In 2009, the Atlanta Woman's Club gave the Carter Center a generous gift to become a partner in our efforts to eradicate the debilitating, painful Guinea worm disease that impacts the poorest people on earth. We began this project in 1986 when there were 3.5 million people afflicted. Today, there are slightly over 1,000 cases of the Guinea worm disease left in the world, those cases primarily in four African countries (Sudan, Ghana, Mali, and Ethiopia) with the majority of cases in Southern Sudan. The Carter Center has been the beneficiary of gifts from large corporations and institutions; we are grateful for contributions like the ones from the AWC that remind us that the spirit of the American people is very much alive.

We have worked tirelessly toward a peaceful world, free from disease and poverty, in which we all strive to protect our natural resources. You will see in the following pages that the AWC has been working toward these same goals since 1895.

We invite you to read this exciting presentation of actions women have taken to make a difference in their community and world. We are happy to write this foreword and offer it as a tribute to all those strong and courageous members of the Atlanta Woman's Club who have gone before, those who have given of their time and energy, and those who have helped make Atlanta and the world a better place. Knowing that there is still much to be done in attaining our goals, we wish the Atlanta Woman's Club continued success in their progress toward bettering the lives of all people.

—Rosalynn and Jimmy Carter

INTRODUCTION

by Former AWC President Karen M. Thomson

It is the late 1860s, only a few years since the end of the Civil War. Women all over the country are struggling under the severely limiting and rigid strictures of nineteenth-century American society, which is closed in so many ways to women. The gifted journalist and women's rights advocate, Mrs. Jane Croly of New York, is stung by insulting treatment and blatantly unreasonable exclusionary customs of a male-dominated society. Over the next twenty years, she and others courageously work to form a women's group, the General Federation of Women's Clubs (GFWC), which comes to fruition in 1890. At a council meeting of the GFWC in Atlanta in 1895, it is decided to start the first GFWC-affiliated club in Georgia. The Atlanta Woman's Club is founded on 11 November 1895. This book begins with the story of "Jennie June" (Mrs. Croly), a story that serves to preface the history of the Atlanta Woman's Club.

 first proposed the idea for this book in my May 2008 acceptance speech as I began a two-year term as president of the Atlanta Woman's Club. From concept to completion, *A Light on Peachtree: A History of the Atlanta Woman's Club* has been four years in the making.

As the Club's archives had been decimated by two fires and the ravages of time, the AWC History Book Committee at first thought there was a poverty of historical information and documentation. However, as our journey with our author then took us to the Kenan Research Center at the Atlanta History Center, we found many exciting details about our history, a discovery that greatly buoyed our enthusiasm. Then, we traveled to Georgia Archives in Morrow, to Tallulah Falls School in North Georgia, and to Georgia State University, which now houses the annals of the Atlanta newspapers. We happily discovered at the Atlanta History Center that the Atlanta Woman's Club (AWC) was featured often and prominently in *The Atlanta Constitution* and *The Atlanta Journal,* particularly from our beginnings through the 1960s.

We were astounded and thrilled to find the original yearbooks and carefully created, bulging scrapbooks containing a wealth of newspaper clippings, letters, agendas, and pictures. These give a clear picture of AWC women and their increasingly progressive and highly influential activities. We have been inspired, amazed, and humbled as we learned from our research of the women's strength, farsightedness, intelligence, diligence, and business sense—particularly considering that this was a time well before women entered the business and work force. Their selfless service, grounded in humanitarian concern and the desire to do good in the world, is evidenced throughout the writings and activities of our founders, leaders, and members from the early decades of the twentieth century and beyond. Although AWC leaders and members ourselves, we had little concept of our history prior to the discoveries in our research. This fact made us all the more dedicated to the task of writing and publishing this history so that it could be brought to light, made available, and easily known and shared.

The fall 1895 International Cotton States Exposition, held in what is now Atlanta's Piedmont Park, brought luminaries from all over the world to Atlanta. It was this event, coupled with the GFWC council meeting, that proved to be the catalyst for the founding of the AWC, the first Georgia woman's club and the oldest GFWC woman's club in Georgia. In 1896, Atlanta Woman's Club members and others helped found the Georgia Federation of Women's Clubs (GaFWC). Rebecca Douglas Lowe, the founding AWC president who was also the founding president of GaFWC, was truly an outstanding woman. She went on to serve two terms as the international GFWC president.

Although Atlanta was a small rural town in 1895, the history of the Atlanta Woman's Club should not be thought of as a provincial club history. Rather, the Club's history represents, metaphorically, in microcosm, and by extension, the history of modern women—in Atlanta, the nation, and the world—as we have sought to find our voices, claim our power, and take action to uplift all women and, in fact, all people.

We are fortunate that photographs of all sixty-seven presidents of the Atlanta Woman's Club, from 1895 to 2012, exist. The pictures have long been displayed in the hall leading downstairs to the Club's ballroom, and they all appear in this volume, thanks to our photographer's work in scanning, digitizing, and editing. Images in this book, too, include an early photograph of an approximately thirty-member AWC Chorus in 1895, pictures from the Club's 1945 50th birthday celebration, and current pictures of our Executive Board and the Board of Trustees. Further, we have included images of some of the current members who have played key roles and made truly significant contributions. Pictures in this volume include some of the art hanging in the Club, such as oil paintings by member and Atlanta attorney-artist-author-opera singer Emily Grigsby, who donated to the Club several of her paintings. We have also included photographs of the Wimbish House, outside and inside, and of the AWC Auditorium, which no longer exists in its original form.

2010 AWC Board of Trustees, Wimbish House. Front (left to right): Sandra McNeil; Karen Bacheller, President 2010-2012; Myra Carmon, BOT Chair 2011-2013. Back (left to right): Karen Clydesdale, BOT Chair 2009-2011; Beth Jetha; Bonnie Kent; Karen Thomson, President 2008-2010; Judine Heard. Absent from photo: Bobbie Kraus.   *Photographer: Aryc W. Mosher*

The book, further, features pictures taken at the April 2010 Spring Tea. Our annual Spring Tea and Open House is always held in April, and it is our tradition that members don hats and festive spring attire and invite their families and potential members to this event to learn more about who we are and what we do. Guests are invited to tour the house where we hold our monthly meetings (September through June). The rooms are adorned with spring flowers, and there are beautifully decorated tables spread with delicious hors d'oeuvres and desserts. In the background elegant piano selections are played by members on our Steinway and Mason & Hamlin grand pianos. Later, a trio of musicians plays chamber music on the ballroom stage. Typically, invited guests, too, include representatives from GaFWC and Tallulah Falls School. In attendance at our 2010 tea was GFWC international president Dr. Rose Ditto, and in 2011, the Georgia governor's wife Mrs. Sandra Deal.

One of the historical gems this book details is our club house, a magnificent mansion in what was during the early 1900s a prestigious neighborhood on Peachtree Street on the outskirts of Atlanta. By virtue of Atlanta's phenomenal growth during the past 100 years, the house, still standing on its original site, is now located in Midtown, close to the busy corner of Peachtree and 14th Street. Surrounded by corporate skyscrapers, trendy restaurants, and upscale hotels, it is just two blocks south of the Woodruff Arts Center and a couple blocks north of the Margaret Mitchell House. Built at the turn of the twentieth century and listed on the historical registry, the Chateauesque-style house was designed by well-known eclectic Atlanta architect Walter T. Downing for prominent Atlanta attorney William Wimbish and his wife. The design was inspired by their friends' sandstone French

2010 AWC Executive Board, Wimbish House. Seated (left to right): Betty Daniels, Lucy Willard, Sarah Helen Killgore, Louise Vernon, Karen Thomson (Pres.). Standing (left to right): Judine Heard, Sandra McNeil, Ellen Milholland, Myra Carmon, Bonnie Kent, Jill Muir, Lisa Banes, Daisy Luckey Aukerman, Ruth Yurchuck, Karen Bacheller, Beth Jetha. Absent from photo: Karen Clydesdale, BOT Chair; Donna Foland; Pat Walsh; and Carrieann Banacki-Gillert.   *Photographer: Aryc W. Mosher*

chalet, which they visited during their wedding trip to France in the late 1890s. The Wimbishes occupied the home from 1906–1919, when they moved to Washington, DC. The reader will enjoy the book's description of how the members of the Atlanta Woman's Club made the astute decision to purchase the home for their clubhouse. Following immediate renovations, the AWC held its first meeting in the house in February 1920, and the Wimbish House has been home to the Atlanta Woman's Club ever since. A banquet hall (now referred to as the Ballroom) was added in 1923, and the Lucille King Thomas Auditorium was added in 1922.

The AWC has had enormous impact on life in Atlanta, and it has touched many people's lives. In the first few decades of its existence, for example, the Club took on the challenges of prison reform, child labor laws, public kindergartens, women's rights, and compulsory education.

In addition, for approximately seventy years, the Atlanta Woman's Club, a hub of cultural activity, was drawing world-class artists to the stage of what was commonly referred to as the "Woman's Club Auditorium" (the Lucille King Thomas Auditorium) and attracting audiences from throughout the South. As one will read in the following pages, the Auditorium, created for women's voices, was described in *The Atlanta Journal* in the 1920s as "the South's most complete auditorium, gem-like in its beauty. . . . It surpasses in cost of erection and beauty every other women's club auditorium in the United States . . . [and] stands foremost as a conspicuous achievement of the club women . . . [and is] one of the most unique buildings in America." It was acoustically advanced, elegant but simple, and the site for numerous concerts, operas, recitals, plays, lectures, meetings, and performances, especially prior to the 1968 opening of the Woodruff Arts Center housing the High Museum, the Atlanta Symphony, and the Arts Alliance Theater. In its last years, the Auditorium served as home for Peachtree Playhouse and Theater of the Stars. Again, the Auditorium no longer exists in its original purpose and design, and we are fortunate to have two pictures included in this book taken inside the Auditorium before its total transformation in the late 1980s.

A faculty colleague, Dr. R. Wayne Gibson, former head of the Kennesaw State College (now Kennesaw State University) Music Department, played key roles in two KSU opera performances (Monteverdi's *Orfeo* and Rossini's *The Marriage of Figaro*), which were among the last operas performed in the Woman's Club Auditorium in the late 1980s. When I told him I was working on our history, he shared a childhood memory of a recital he attended in the auditorium: "One of my most prominent memories is of a recital in the fifties by Hilde Gueden, Viennese soprano. I was just a kid and had never been that close to a real, live, world-class soprano. It was spectacular, and I remember that she sang 'Sempre libera' from *Traviata* as an encore, I believe. She sang it marvelously, and in the middle of the fastest part, the pianist, while furiously turning a page, threw his music all over the stage. He, of course, finished the piece without a hitch—from memory. That was thrilling for a teenaged Wayne." My sister, Ki, remembers as a teenager dancing in the Auditorium with other students from the Atlanta School of Ballet led by the legendary "Miss Dorothy" Alexander, who was their teacher. I, too, remember attending concerts in the Auditorium while in high school in the early sixties.

In the late 1980s, AWC members made the business-savvy decision to lease the Auditorium to renters, who would then change the Auditorium into a night club. Today, what was once the Auditorium offering cultural experiences to Atlantans has been transformed into a flourishing nightclub known as "Opera" and remodeled to look like a nineteenth-century opera house. In the summer of 2008, it was voted the "Best Dance Club in Atlanta," and today it continues to bring national and world celebrities to its stage.

The leasing of both the Auditorium as a night club and the Wimbish House as a venue for weddings and other special events provides the income for the AWC not only to maintain the house, but also to fund the numerous philanthropic and humanitarian causes in which the AWC participates. This income precludes the need for club fundraisers.

As we look over the long history of the Atlanta Woman's Club, we find that our contributions and concerns in the first few decades frequently took us into uncharted territory and not only served to expand our concept of what we as women could do but also helped broaden Atlanta's societal perceptions of women and the work they could do and do well. For decades, the AWC was, in fact, the place outside of the home, family, and church where many women could channel their energy, talents, and abilities into community service. Beginning in 1920, the Wimbish House was the AWC members' home away from home. The early leaders cared deeply about educating and broadening the horizons of their members. They provided stimulating educational programs, hosted speakers on varied subjects, housed a library of thousands of carefully selected books, and supported the first art gallery in Atlanta. They also provided for women's physical and social activities by maintaining a swimming pool and tennis courts.

In its quest to educate and uplift others, AWC extended concern for women from rural areas and for children. At times AWC membership reached 1,000 to 1,400 members. No doubt, in part due to the work of the AWC members and others of like mind, society has changed and opened its doors in multitudinous ways. Today we have many choices in our lives compared to what was available to us in 1895, when we could not vote, when we were barred from attending state-supported colleges and universities such as Georgia Tech or the University of Georgia, and when, for most women, having a professional life was essentially not an option. Perhaps because we have so many opportunities to choose from, our AWC membership numbers today around sixty members.

This book is merely a beginning in detailing our history in that there is more information available than this book was ever intended to present. Those of us who participated in the research—the four-member AWC Book Committee plus our author—like to believe there will be a subsequent volume that will continue to share even more of our history held in the aforementioned locations of our research.

As with most worthwhile projects, this book has necessarily taken more time than ever anticipated and exists because many came forward to provide assistance along the way. First, I must acknowledge with supreme appreciation both our author and AWC member, Anne B. Jones, Ph.D., and our photographer, Aryc W. Mosher, who have generously given of their time, energy, and professional expertise. We are extremely fortunate that these individuals stepped forward to take on the lion's share of this project without regard or desire for compensation. Their work, as represented in these pages, is their gift to the Atlanta Woman's Club, and without them, this book would not exist. Our immense gratitude goes out to each of them.

We are, also, very fortunate and deeply honored to have the involvement of former President and Mrs. Jimmy Carter, who have written the book's foreword, which is most befitting, it seems, as they have devoted their lives to humanitarian concern and world service. To the Carters, to the Carter Center, and to Becky Brookshire and Aryc Mosher, both of the Carter Center, we sincerely thank you for your superb efforts. How terrific, also, to have the International General Federation of Women's Clubs president, 2008–2010, Dr. Rose Ditto, to write our epilogue. Again, we are honored by her participation. Pictures of her visit from GFWC international headquarters in Washington, DC, as our special guest at the April 2010 AWC Spring Tea appear in this book. Our thanks to Rose!

It is with infinite gratitude that I offer thanks to others who provided support and assistance in numerous ways in the creation of this book: Drs. Dede and John Yow; Dr. Candace Kaspers; Chuck Perry; Laurie Shock; Dr. Marc Jolley and Marsha Luttrell of Mercer University Press; Tim Ste. Marie and Dr. Teresa Joyce of Kennesaw

The Light in the Mountains is a framed reproduction of the original art created for Tallulah Falls School and presented to the Atlanta Woman's Club for contributions to the school during their one hundredth birthday celebration in 2009. It hangs upstairs in the Wimbish House. *Photographer: Aryc W. Mosher*

State University Press; Sue VerHoef and the staff at the Kenan Research Center of the Atlanta History Center; Jaclyn Sinclair; Bob Land; Kay and Dudley Ottley, descendants of Mrs. J.K. Ottley (AWC's second president, 1896–1897, and, by 1922, working director of the board and then president of the Board of Trustees at Tallulah Falls School); Dr. Mary Zoghby; Dr. Gloria Henderson; John Brieske at the *AJC*, who found the newspaper clippings confirming that Houdini gave a lecture at the AWC in 1924; and Don Russell Clayton, who not only gifted the Club with two Athos Menaboni lithographs in 2011 that now hang in the Wimbish House, but also introduced us to the paintings of Wilbur Kurtz (one of which hung for decades over the fireplace in the Wimbish House living room beginning in the 1920s) who, with his wife, spoke on several occasions to the Club about his role as historical consultant on *Gone with the Wind*.

Deep gratitude, also, goes to those associated with the Atlanta Woman's Club: our AWC attorney, Jennifer Chapin, who has always provided expert counsel and guidance and has done so during this project; our AWC event coordinator, Beth Beery, who helps us at every turn, and has done so here; and to AWC members— Judine Heard, who transcribed taped interviews and meetings; First Lady of Tallulah Falls School and AWC member and Second Vice President Dinah Peevy, who facilitated research at TFS; and longstanding members and extraordinary contributors to AWC who have shared so much of their hearts and lives with the AWC, and who recalled for us memories in taped interviews and loaned us treasured materials: Daisy Luckey Aukerman, Sarah Helen Killgore, Sandra McNeil, Louise Vernon, and Lucy Willard.

To the AWC History Book Committee—AWC president, Karen Bacheller; former Board of Trustees chair, Karen Clydesdale; and Public Issues chair, Lisa Banes—my thanks for your diligence, persistence, perseverance, and utmost kindness throughout this process.

I would be remiss not to extend deep appreciation to my dear husband Tom, who provided invaluable assistance throughout this four-year process with his recorded interviews of members and an AWC general meeting that focused on historical recollections, creating DVDs from the interviews and meeting, and, finally, preparing the manuscript and photographs for publication and mailing, as well as assisting in proofreading.

Finally, it is the women of the Atlanta Woman's Club, past and present, who are responsible for this history. The early women used as their motto and the title of their yearbooks "More Light." That motto and title changed over the years to "Light, More Light." Tallulah Falls School is often referred to as a "light in the mountains," as attested to by their published history book, *A Light in the Mountains: The Story of Tallulah Falls School* by Carol Stevens Hancock (1975/1990). In the time-honored literary sense, "light" is used to symbolize all that is positive: love, joy, grace, peace, beauty, wisdom, strength, etc.—a powerful force of goodness in this world. Because of our close connection with Tallulah Falls School as "the light in the mountains," the nature of our work, our location on Peachtree Street, and the symbolism associated with light, we chose the title *A Light on Peachtree: A History of the Atlanta Woman's Club*.

It is with pleasure that we present our history here, offered as a tribute to our predecessors. It is our hope that it inspires and informs modern readers and attracts contemporary Atlanta women who, in understanding something of our history and mission, will join us in our work. Just as AWC members of the past brought "Light" and "More Light" to our city, our desire is to continue their legacy so that the Atlanta Woman's Club remains a torch, a beacon, "a Light on Peachtree" dedicated to local and global humanitarian, philanthropic service.

—Karen M. Thomson, Ph.D.
President, Atlanta Woman's Club, 2008–2010
Director, AWC History Book Project
Chair, AWC History Book Committee, 2008–2012

In many parlors, large and small, across a nation that itself was expanding and changing, women were asking, "Is it possible?"

Mary Jean Houde[1]

The roots of the Atlanta Woman's Club began in 1868, when, because she was a woman, New York writer Jane Cunningham Croly was refused admission to a dinner given by the Press Club of New York at Delmonico's Restaurant honoring novelist Charles Dickens. When Horace Greeley, editor of the *New York Tribune*, declined to preside over the meeting unless Croly and other women were welcome, it was finally agreed they could attend seated behind a curtain or out of sight. Justifiably insulted, Jane Croly declined the invitation.

Neither she, nor those who impeded her, could have dreamed of the ramifications of that incident. Spurred by the degrading experience, Mrs. Croly set off a chain of actions that opened doors not only for women, but also for children, the sick and disabled, those who suffered injustice and those who, due to circumstances beyond their control, could not provide for themselves. Major efforts would be channeled into education and the humanities, fostering public support, and encouraging the development of scholars, writers, artists, dramatists, and musicians. These thunderous forthcoming events spread beyond New York, throughout every state, and eventually had an impact on the world.

Already empowered by her pen, "Jennie June," as Mrs. Croly was known by her pseudonym, had long been a proponent of women's welfare. She was married to journalist David Croly, with whom she had five children. Well respected and known for her journalistic ability, she wrote

---

1 Mary Jean Houde, *Reaching Out: A Story of the General Federation of Women's Clubs* (Washington/Chicago: Mobium Press, 1989) 1.

Early undated picture of Atlanta Woman's Club members

2 Ibid., 1–5.

3 "World History and Geography," *Student's Friend*, www.students friend.com (accessed 24 September 2009).

hundreds of articles for women specializing in human interest. One of her notable achievements was to have become a pioneer syndicated columnist whose works were read nationwide. Mrs. Croly quickly realized what could be achieved by spreading knowledge through the power of her pen and by helping readers develop their potential. She wondered what might result if they could exchange ideas and combine their talents in unison.

At the time, women were looked upon as second-class citizens who, like children, should be seen but not heard. They were not allowed to vote, take part in major political events, or speak in public groups.[2]

Despite this backwardness, a spiraling increase in technological change had thrown the nation into a state of flux. Most people still farmed and traveled old dirt roads in buggies and wagons, but now there were trains. The telephone soon made communication almost instantaneous, but regional and economic differences were accentuated by an uneasy peace following the Civil War and by the contrasts between isolated and mainstream geographic areas.

The United States followed old-world patterns of industrialization and expansion, sparking conflict as it conquered Native American nations and Mexican armies. The Spanish-American War loomed on the horizon and questions about foreign policy, and our relationships with other countries, created tension.[3] However, in spite of ominous threats of domestic and foreign warfare, the residents of Georgia and the rest of our country were mainly concerned with daily survival. Many could not read, and only the privileged were formally educated. One-room schoolhouses dotted the countryside, led by teachers who had little, if any, training and taught limited basic skills related to reading, writing, and math. Into this turbulent mix, Jane Croly bravely set forth, calling women to action in a centralized force, beginning in New York, and then, with a cry echoing in the hearts of women, in Georgia and throughout the nation.

CHAPTER TWO

For the city of Atlanta and its women, as for the South as a whole, the Civil War was clearly the turning point. Both southern myth and southern reality were altered by the struggle.... Just as Atlanta's revival from the war marks its true origin as an industrial leader of the New South, the experience of the war marks the emergence of new images and realities for its women. After the war, southern women found themselves in familiar surroundings, but the "old place" now had unrecognizable social formations.

Darlene Rebecca Roth[4]

uring 1868, the same year Jane Croly was discouraged from attending the meeting in Delmonico's restaurant, Atlanta newspaper editor Henry W. Grady was invited to New York to speak at Delmonico's during a banquet. Also attending was William Tecumseh Sherman, the hated general who had burned Atlanta during the Civil War.

During the latter half of the century, Georgia was in a difficult fight to rebuild, and life was hard. Grady, a respected newspaperman and visionary, urged the South to look forward and seek prosperity and greatness by tapping into its human and natural resources rather than focusing on loss and bitterness. Reaching out to the North and the South to encourage healing, he became a symbol of national unity. At the same time, he promoted Georgia's development, calling for the state to manufacture its own products and limit shipments of raw materials to other regions.[5] Grady's attendance at Delmonico's signaled change.

4 Roth, *Matronage: Patterns In Women's Organizations, Atlanta, Georgia, 1890–1940* (Brooklyn: Carlson Publishing, 1994) 20.

5 McCuller, *This Is Your Georgia* (Woodville AL: Viewpoint Publications, 1986) 178–83.

6 Houde, *Reaching Out: A Story of the General Federation of Women's Clubs* (Washington/Chicago: Mobium Press, 1989) 1–7.

Grady was envisioning a progressive role for Georgia while Jane Croly was envisioning a progressive role for women. Neither was aware their visions would eventually converge.

During that same year, in defiance of social norms, Mrs. Croly formed a woman's club whose goal was to empower women through unity. The club's first members, conscious many would condemn the notion of women meeting for common purposes, recognized the importance of the Club's name in influencing public opinion. After much discussion, Mrs. Croly suggested the Greek word *Sorosis*. Among the definitions that emerged was "a cluster of flowers on one stem," which, in club language, refers to members attached to the whole. The word was also defined as an "aggregation, a sweet flavor of many fruits, as in the pineapple," which soon became the Club's symbol. The formation of the Sorosis Club was a huge step for women in the climate of the times and a foreshadowing of things to come.

As one of the nation's most highly regarded women, Croly had access to other prominent women. Her greatest ability as a writer was gathering and weaving diverse resources, and she transferred those talents into club work. From the beginning, she invited members and officers who had the contacts, money, and ability to promote elegance and prestige. She sought those who garnered respect and acceptance by men and women alike, while providing a variety of talents and intellect. By seeking out women of accomplishment and status, she gave the Club credibility.

The Crolys hosted two preliminary meetings at their home, but, ironically, the Sorosis Club held its first regular meeting at Delmonico's. The Club's stated purposes included providing opportunities for women to become acquainted; to work and learn together; to reach out to larger aims; to promote relationships among women of literary and artistic taste, independent of sectionalism or partisanship; to recognize women of thought, culture, and humanity; and to teach women to think for themselves. The meetings afforded an opportunity for women to discuss social and intellectual topics, the results of which would soon exert influence on the future and welfare of women throughout the United States, including Georgia.

Considering the social standards of the time and the lack of respect for women's intellectual contributions, it was no surprise that the Sorosis Club was met with scorn. However, its members were not discouraged. Membership reached eighty-three during the first year and included artists, authors, editors, poets, teachers, lecturers, philanthropists, physicians, science writers, a historian, and others who contributed to periodicals.[6]

At the same time the Sorosis Club became active, many other women's clubs were taking root. Some were loosely structured and simply offered friendship and support to women in isolated rural and western communities. Others were already performing public service and working for social reform, such as prohibition and women's suffrage. The clubs varied dramatically in the class and education of their members, yet they provided nurturing for personal development while becoming avenues to community involvement.

As the number of clubs and members expanded, Croly's thoughts about unity grew. What if women from all over the country could learn from and support each other? What if they were bound together in a unified whole? Again, using her creativity and the power of her pen, she set about to transform her thoughts into reality. As interactions between clubs occurred, women echoed her question: What if we all came together?

Reformer Julia Ward Howe, an honorary member of the Sorosis Club and leader of the New England Woman's Club of Boston, stated, "It occurred to them that union is strength. A new power is now making itself felt among women, the power of associated action."[7] In 1888, Jennie June made a motion that Sorosis convene a Convention of Clubs. The motion passed, and a call was issued to all known clubs throughout the nation. Caught up in the moment and filled with grand hopes, women from every region of the country answered, including the women of Georgia.[8]

[7] Houde, *Reaching Out*, 17.

[8] Ibid., 19.

CHAPTER THREE

During the late nineteenth and early twentieth centuries, American women awakened to the power of their voices and the strength of their collective organization through the woman's club movement.

Athens Woman's Club[9]

y 1889, women in Atlanta and throughout the United States were poised to help shape the new millennium and consequently were forming more clubs. Their efforts were set against a background of unprecedented inventive and industrial activity, new freedom for intellectual thought, ever-expanding travel and communication, and unlimited hope for the future.[10] In spring 1889, under Jane Croly's guidance, the Sorosis Club held a "Conference to Form a Permanent Federation of Clubs" in New York with an opening reception at Delmonico's. Among the Club's goals were the exchange of information and the development of a plan to organize the nation's diverse clubs into a unified whole.[11]

Filled with anticipation, energy and recognition of the power of their ideas, the women made plans and shared their experiences. Ella Dietz Clymer was named chairman of a committee to unify the independent clubs, and she began by expressing gratitude. She thanked the women for coming long distances from all regions of the nation, stating, "We look for unity, but unity in diversity." Those words, "Unity in Diversity," became the new organization's motto.[12]

9 "For Our Mutual Benefit: The Athens Woman's Club and Social Reform, 1899–1920," date unknown, Athens Woman's Club collection, Heritage Room, Athens-Clarke County Library, Athens GA, from the Digital Library of Georgia/GALILEO (Athens GA: University of Georgia Libraries, 2006–2007), dlg.galileo.usg.edu/athenswomansclub (accessed 23 October 2009).

10 Houde, *Reaching Out: A Story of the General Federation of Women's Clubs* (Washington/Chicago: Mobium Press, 1989) 17.

11 Ibid., 20–21.

12 Ibid., 26–27.

13 Ibid., 23–24.

14 Ibid., 1–7.

15 Ibid., 54; "Cotton Expositions in Atlanta," *History and Archaeology*, New Georgia Encyclopedia, www.georgia encyclopedia.org/nge/Article.jsp?id= h-2913 (accessed 25 October 2009).

16 Houde, *Reaching Out*, 42–44.

17 Ibid., 44–45.

18 Ibid., 53–65.

19 Staman, *Loosening Corsets* (Macon GA: Tiger Iron Press, 2006) 111–12; Atlanta History Center book (43,).

The discussions were so intense and information so forthcoming that the convention was extended a fourth day. Such a powerful, energetic, and eclectic gathering of women was never before seen. Within a short time, hundreds of women's clubs joined, and the General Federation of Women's Clubs became an important force in the women's rights movement—with one caveat. Jane Croly believed that before women became voters, they must become educated.[13] Armed with a formidable growing membership of thinkers, in just over twenty-one years, the Sorosis Club had evolved into a national federation that would become one of the largest club organizations of women volunteers in the world.[14]

While women were bonding together for strength, other important opportunities and events were taking place. During the latter half of the 1800s, as Atlanta, Georgia, and the nation looked toward the future, several important fairs and expositions focused attention on the country's natural resources, technological developments, and new industrial products. These expositions attracted visitors from all over the world. Among the most well publicized and widely attended was the 1893 Chicago World's Columbian Exposition.[15]

One of the most influential and accomplished Chicago clubs taking part in the Exposition was the Chicago Woman's Club, which saw its involvement as an opportunity to educate its visitors to women's expanding roles and potential. Jane Croly once referred to the Chicago Woman's Club as a modern department club, with reform, home, education, philanthropy, art and literature, and philosophy and science departments. Its example became manifest in the GFWC's organization, with member clubs' inclusion of similar departments. The club was among the first participants in the General Federation and included such esteemed members as Jane Addams, a proponent of social reform and cofounder of Hull House, a settlement house for newly arrived immigrants.[16]

In 1892, the Chicago Woman's Club hosted the first biennial convention of the General Federation of Women's Clubs. The gathering was an opportunity to push for the formation of GFWC state federations, to involve other clubs in the planning of a Woman's Building at the Chicago Exposition, and to encourage attendance at the World Congress of Women, which was to be held simultaneously.[17] Among the most prominent Southern clubs to attend the convention was the Woman's Press Club of Georgia.[18] The involvement and recognition of women in the planning of the Chicago Exposition and many expositions to follow was due to the hard work of women's rights activists, particularly woman's suffrage advocate Susan B. Anthony. Ms. Anthony conceived of and created the Exposition's Board of Lady Managers. Serving as business manager for the Woman's Division was Georgia activist Rebecca Latimer Felton, who would later become an influential speaker at the Atlanta Woman's Club, a member of the Georgia Federation of Women's Clubs and General Federation of Women's Clubs, and the nation's first female senator. At the time of the Exposition, Mrs. Felton's duties included locating and placing the women's exhibits and keeping an eye on the division's finances. Little did she realize her work would not only profoundly impact the Chicago Exposition but, along with the efforts of other women, would also lead to unfathomable opportunities for women in her home state of Georgia.[19]

The Exposition was successful beyond expectations. Along with viewing the women's exhibits, visitors and clubwomen networked, and their frequent contacts made the event a springboard for club expansion.[20] Beginning in 1881, several lesser expositions were promoted by Henry Grady and others in the Georgia Confederacy and, by 1895, preparations were being made for a Cotton States and International Exposition to be held in Atlanta in fall 1895 and to last over three months.[21]

In January that year, Susan B. Anthony arrived in Atlanta to preside over the twenty-seventh annual gathering of the National American Woman's Suffrage Association. The event was held in DeGive's Opera House at Forsyth and Marietta streets, a site that would soon serve as home to a new and courageous organization known as the Atlanta Woman's Club. Before Ms. Anthony arrived, she gave an interview to the *New York Sun* in which she said, "A story is always repeating itself. There is going to be a second 'Marching Through Georgia' but this time it will be women on a mission of peace and not men in the smoke and suffering of war." Her presence had a profound impact on the women of Atlanta and throughout the South.[22]

Patterned after the Chicago Exposition, the Cotton States and International Exposition also included a Women's Department, a Board of Women's Managers, and a Women's Building. The Women's Building was designed by female architect Elsie Mercer of Pittsburgh in the graceful Colonial Renaissance style. Its $35,000 cost was contributed by the women of Atlanta, who raised the money through a variety of means including entertainments, fairs, and bazaars. One of their most unusual and notable efforts was a woman's edition of *The Atlanta Journal*.[23] The Women's Department was one of the most active and effective organizations connected with the Cotton States Exposition.[24]

Most Southern states had responded slowly to the General Federation of Women's Clubs movement. In an attempt to foster the establishment of Southern state federations, the GFWC accepted an invitation from the Women's Board of Managers and the Georgia Woman's Press Club to host a Federation Day at the Women's Building. Clubwomen from all over the country attended, networking, exchanging stories, and sharing their experiences with their GFWC state federations. The event was enthusiastically received, and within two years Georgia, Alabama, Tennessee, Arkansas, and Florida established their own federations.[25]

Many states and cities were also granted specific days for activities during the Cotton States Exposition, and Georgia's was scheduled for November 19. Along with an array of esteemed gentlemen, Rebecca Latimer Felton was invited to speak in a tribute to Henry W. Grady. Colonel Albert H. Cox of Atlanta spoke at the request of the Board of Women's Managers. His wife, who was on the board and on the Household Economics Committee, later became a charter member in the organization of the Atlanta Woman's Club.[26]

As had been the case in Chicago, the Atlanta exposition's Woman's Department was described as one of the event's most successful participants. The Women's Building housed exhibits representing almost every art and industry in which women engaged, and there were opportunities for meetings and interaction with many outstanding women speakers.[27] The women were so energized and compelling

[20] Houde, *Reaching Out*, 53–65.

[21] McCullar, *This Is Your Georgia* (Woodville AL: Viewpoint Publications, 1986) 183; *Cotton States and International Exposition (1895)*, retrieved 25 Oct 2009 from http:/en.wikipedia.org/wiki/Cotton_States_and_International_Exposition_1895.

[22] Garrett, *Atlanta and Environs: A Chronicle of Its People and Events* (New York: Lewis Historical Pub. Co., 1954, 1987) 2:310; Staman, *Loosening Corsets*, 111–12.

[23] Garrett, *Atlanta and Environs*, 324; Cooper, *History of Fulton County* (Atlanta: History Commission, 1934) 424.

[24] Garrett, *Atlanta and Environs*, 315.

[25] Houde, *Reaching Out*, 71; "For Our Mutual Benefit."

[26] Garrett, *Atlanta and Environs*, 315; notes from 1895 scrapbook, Atlanta Woman's Club Scrapbook Collection, MSS 326–60, Kenan Research Center, Atlanta History Center, Atlanta GA.

[27] Garrett, *Atlanta and Environs*, 2:315–24.

28 Ibid.; notes from 1895 scrapbook, *Atlanta Woman's Club Scrapbook Collection.*

29 Notes from 1895 scrapbook, *Atlanta Woman's Club Scrapbook Collection.*

that they had a profound influence on everyone who entered, including one of the most wealthy and intelligent women of Atlanta, Rebecca Douglas Lowe.[28]

Only months before, Mrs. Lowe had declined an important chairmanship on the Women's Board of Managers for the Cotton States Exposition because she felt she was not ready to devote herself to outside work. However, she was so inspired by her experience at the Women's Building that she enthusiastically changed her mind, embraced the philosophy of the woman's club movement, and prepared herself for action.[29]

CHAPTER FOUR

[The Atlanta Woman's Club] gives the young women a sensible and improving way of occupying time that would otherwise be spent, perhaps in the consummation of chocolate creams, which are bad for the complexion, or in meaning-less flirtations, which are bad for the heart.

Atlanta Constitution, 1896

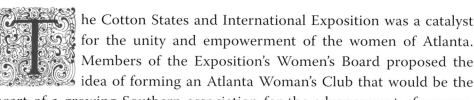he Cotton States and International Exposition was a catalyst for the unity and empowerment of the women of Atlanta. Members of the Exposition's Women's Board proposed the idea of forming an Atlanta Woman's Club that would be the heart of a growing Southern association for the advancement of women. The idea quickly received support from Rebecca Douglas Lowe and other thinking women of the city, and the day after the adjournment of the General Federation Board of Directors, Jane Croly and other organization leaders met at Mrs. Lowe's home to discuss the matter.[30]

In late 1895, "With some fear and considerable misgiving, a group of progressive Atlanta women met at Rebecca Douglas Lowe's Peachtree Street home near North Avenue to discuss the advisability of forming an organization to be known as the Atlanta Woman's Club. The object of the Club was to be the bringing together of the women of the city, women in all walks of life, for the purpose of good fellowship, better understanding and social contact." The club's mission "was also to prove to the world that women could participate in civic, philanthropic and legislative interests, and in standing side by side with the development of the times, could aid in

---

30 "Woman's Club an Assured Success," unidentified newspaper clipping, 1895 *Atlanta Woman's Club Scrapbook Collection*, MSS 326–60, Kenan Research Center, Atlanta History Center, Atlanta GA; "Atlanta Woman's Club," paper from the General Federation of Women's Clubs Federation Archives, 11 November 1895; Houde, *Reaching Out: A Story of the General Federation of Women's Clubs* (Washington/Chicago: Mobium Press, 1989) 71.

31 Garrett, *Atlanta and Environs: A Chronicle of Its People and Events* (New York: Lewis Historical Pub. Co., 1954, 1987) 2:340.

32 "Woman's Club an Assured Success," unidentified newspaper clipping, 1895 scrapbook, *Atlanta Woman's Club Scrapbook Collection*, MSS 326–60, Kenan Research Center, Atlanta History Center; "Atlanta Woman's Club" paper from the General Federation of Women's Clubs Federation Archives, Wimbish House Archives.

33 Notes, "Atlanta Woman's Club, November 11th, 1895," 1895 scrapbook, *Atlanta Woman's Club Scrapbook Collection*, MSS 326–60.

34 Notes, 1895 *Atlanta Woman's Club Scrapbook Collection*, MSS 326–60.

35 Ibid.

36 Ibid.

37 Ibid.

38 "Form," 1895 *Atlanta Woman's Club Scrapbook Collection*, MSS 326–60.

the progress of a great city, with an earnestness of purpose, combining of efforts and a unity of thought characteristic of womankind."[31]

To the casual observer, the Atlanta Woman's Club may have simply been the result of overzealous women who had experienced favor and recognition at Atlanta's recent Cotton States and International Exposition, the Southern equivalent of a world's fair. But the seeds of the Club, planted nearly three decades earlier in the Sorosis Club, were merely sprouting.

The forthcoming club was described as a "natural outburst of the times," and during several meetings in Lowe's home the plans were laid. The diverse group of women attending the first meeting included Jane Croly, who described the "club idea" as one whose greatest work was establishing sisterhood. She discussed the functions and uses of club life and how women could accomplish great things when they worked in unison. A notice posted in the newspaper invited all interested women to an organizational meeting.[32]

The meeting, in which many prominent Atlanta women took part, began with a resolution for organization, followed by a discussion as to the Club's purposes and general characteristics. All were in favor of the organization working to spread the Club's influence along educational, benevolent, and conservative lines and to help the unfortunate. They explored ways to attract other Atlanta women and gain their cooperation. Ultimately, the women gathered at this meeting decided to apply immediately for membership in the General Federation of Women's Clubs.[33]

Since the women felt the Atlanta Woman's Club could not move forward without elected officers, Mrs. Albert Cox nominated Rebecca Douglas Lowe for president: "I wish to nominate a woman who, since the early history of Atlanta, has been closely identified with its progress, a woman who has given her help to every enterprise and has been in hearty sympathy with all that pertained to the city's growth and advancement. I nominate Mrs. William B. Lowe for president of this body."[34]

Lowe modestly accepted, saying she believed the chief quality an executive officer could display during the Club's early months should be earnestness and adding, "That quality I have."[35] The nominations that followed resulted in the election of Mrs. Albert Cox as first vice president; Mrs. James Jackson as second vice president; Mrs. Henry H. Smith as corresponding secretary; Miss Corinne Stocker as seconding secretary; and Mrs. Hugh Hagan as treasurer.[36]

Respected for her business ability and widely known as a woman of brilliance and distinction, Lowe was a conspicuous figure in Southern social life.[37] Well-traveled and cosmopolitan-minded, she was knowledgeable, interested in all educational matters, and an advocate of women's influence in civic affairs.[38] She translated these characteristics into the Club's goals, and they became part of its constitution: "The object of the Club is three-fold," she stated, "social, literary and humanitarian. We wish to bring all of the earnest-minded capable women of Atlanta in a union of common fellowship. There are many women here of fine ability whom it will develop, and who will in turn develop it." She urged the Club to look into all areas of needed reform, including free kindergarten and to "make it a dignified, conservative, forceful body—such as will be a credit to the city and will gain and hold the admira-

Atlanta Woman's Club Chorus, 1895

tion and cooperation of our husbands and sons."[39] The overall objective was to maintain an organized social and civic center among the women of Atlanta, uniting their efforts and mutual interests."[40] The Atlanta Woman's Club's motto is "More Light," an apt commentary on the need for women to be enlightened and to come out of their homes and participate in their community.[41]

Among other topics of conversation were the advantages of the General Federation and issues related to juvenile justice. Mrs. George Leonard Cheney gave such an impassioned plea for support for a separate reformatory prison for youthful criminals that the Club decided to call upon the Georgia Legislature to take immediate action. The women called for the establishment of a separate prison for young convicts, away from the influence of hardened criminals, where they could learn an occupation or trade during their confinement.[42]

At its inception, the Atlanta Woman's Club faced such a prudish Victorian environment and unfavorable public sentiment toward women that many husbands forbade their wives to join. As the Club gained status, male fears diminished and members displayed importance and influence in civic and local affairs: "Beginning with a two dollar initiation fee and two dollars annual dues, the organization quickly attracted over 400 members."[43]

With its burgeoning membership, the clubwomen secured quarters in two rooms on the fifth floor of the DeGive's Opera House (later called the Grand Theater Building). Noting the need for a permanent home, club members established a building fund.[44] Continuing to grow, the Atlanta Woman's Club was often called one of the largest, most successful, most practical, and best conducted bodies of its kind in the South. Although some of the members' interests included both women's rights and politics, the clubwomen preferred not to be considered suffragettes or members of a

39 Notes, 1895 *Atlanta Woman's Club Scrapbook Collection*, MSS 326–60.

40 Atlanta Historical Society Archives, Private Collections Inventory, MSS 353, Kenan Research Center, Atlanta History Center, Atlanta GA.

41 Author unknown, "Through the Years," p. 176, Atlanta Woman's Club Wimbish House Archives, Atlanta GA.

42 Notes, 1895 *Atlanta Woman's Club Scrapbook Collection*, MSS 326–60.

43 "Through the Years," 176.

44 Garrett, *Atlanta and Environs*, 2:34; "History of the Atlanta Woman's Club: Its Growth and Resultful Achievements," *Atlanta Woman's Club Souvenir Book*, pp. 3–7, Wimbish House Archives.

45 Notes, 1895 scrapbook, *Atlanta Woman's Club Scrapbook Collection*, MSS 326–60; "The Atlanta Woman's Club Celebrates 100 Years," *Northside Neighbor*, Wed, 8 Nov 1995, B2.

46 Andy Ambrose, *Atlanta: An Illustrated History* (Athens GA: Hill Street Press, 2003) 91–92.

political group. They focused their attention on learning and the arts, the betterment of their community, and the development of leadership skills.[45]

The Club's counterpart, the Atlanta Federation of Negro Women's Clubs, was formed about the same time. However, due to the political climate, the demands of Jim Crow, and the harsh penalties suffered by those who broke societal taboos, Atlanta's women's organizations were segregated. The restrictions of segregation presented an almost insurmountable obstacle, preventing the joint efforts of women who, in many instances, were seeking the same goals. This separation became more obvious as the clubs channeled energy into social reform.[46]

CHAPTER FIVE

. . .Gentlemen . . . . Do you not see that so long as society says a woman is incompetent to be a lawyer, minister or doctor, but has ample ability to be a teacher, that every man of you who chooses this profession tacitly acknowledges that he has no more brains than a woman?

Susan B. Anthony[47]

he Atlanta Woman's Club's first meeting in the DeGive's Opera House was held 20 January 1896, a little over two months after its organization.[48] From its beginning, the Club emphasized the importance of education and sisterhood, values traced to the first recorded sorority in the United States, which was organized a short distance away in Macon, Georgia.

In 1851, a literary society had been formed at Wesleyan College in Macon. The society later became known as Alpha Delta Pi. About the same time, Philomenthean was founded, also at Wesleyan. Philomenthean evolved into Phi Mu. These sororities (no longer at Wesleyan) were the predecessors of self-education clubs. Their influence was widespread among Wesleyan graduates, many of whom were prominent Atlanta women who became Atlanta Woman's Club members.[49]

Most women's organizations of this period saw motherhood as central to women's roles within their culture, and the Atlanta Woman's Club was no exception.[50] During the late 1890s, many clubs in the General

47 Susan B. Anthony, address, 1853 annual education conference, Rochester NY, spartacus.schoolnet.co.uk/USAWanthony.htm (accessed 7 September 2001).

48 Unidentified news clipping, *Atlanta Constitution*, Feb 1896, 1895 *Atlanta Woman's Club Scrapbook Collection*, MSS 326–60, Kenan Research Center, Atlanta History Center, Atlanta GA; Boutwell, "The Grand Old Lady," newspaper clipping, Wimbish House Archives, Atlanta GA.

49 Roth, *Matronage: Patterns In Women's Organizations, Atlanta, Georgia, 1890–1940* (Brooklyn: Carlson Publishing, 1994) 30–31.

50 Ibid., 4.

51 Unidentified newspaper clipping, 9 Mar 1896, 1895 scrapbook, *Atlanta Woman's Club Scrapbook Collection*; "President Ottley Home Section Hostess," unidentified newspaper clipping, 1895 *Atlanta Woman's Club Scrapbook Collection*, MSS 326–60.

52 "November Notes" and unidentified 1896 newspaper clipping, 1895 scrapbook, *Atlanta Woman's Club Scrapbook Collection*, MSS 326–60.

53 "Woman's Club Meets,"*Atlanta Constitution*, 28 Apr 1896, 1895 *Atlanta Woman's Club Scrapbook Collection*, MSS 326–60.

54 *Atlanta Constitution*, 6 May 1896, 1895 *Atlanta Woman's Club Scrapbook Collection*, MSS 326–60.

55 Unidentified article, *Atlanta Constitution*, 7 June 1896,1895 *Atlanta Woman's Club Scrapbook Collection*, MSS 326–60.

56 Roth, *Matronage*, 4; "Club Women Heartily Second the Move," unidentified newspaper clipping, 1897, in 1895 scrapbook, *Atlanta Woman's Club Scrapbook Collection*, MSS 326–60.

Federation were primarily concerned with issues related to domesticity; however, the women were increasingly hungry for learning, and, as the turn of the century approached, their interests grew, especially in political science and other academic areas. An early 1896 *Atlanta Constitution* newspaper article described the Atlanta Woman's Club as a "force of bright earnest women" that sponsored programs related to music; the mental and moral effects of food; the value of nutrition in warding off disease; and psychology and bacteriology.[51]

Members strongly believed in broadening themselves by being informed about history, the arts, and current issues. The Club found that the quickest way to achieve this was by hosting guest speakers. During the span of a meeting, experts and activists presented capsule versions of courses on a wide variety of subjects. Atlantans were fascinated by this, and the Club's endeavors were frequently reported in the news. A February 1896 *Atlanta Constitution* article described the Club as being like a big college wherein each student could choose the line of study she preferred for intellectual development.

The Atlanta Woman's Club offered opportunities to learn about hygiene, cleaning, child care, cooking, aromatic herbs, philanthropy, and concerns and actions for the unfortunate. Their programs also included poetry, music, citizenship issues, and international affairs, which were discussed in weekly meetings. Members wanted sound, practical knowledge in whatever pertained to human betterment and happiness.[52] During one of the Club's early meetings, people from a variety of charity groups and agencies were invited to talk about their organizations and their concerns. A presentation by a representative of the Salvation Army was so compelling that the Club offered help at once.[53]

The Club's headquarters at the DeGive's Opera House allowed expansive meeting space and opportunities for events on a large and elegant scale. To cite one example, during a convention of the Medical Association, the Club hosted a reception in honor of women involved in the field of medicine, with entertainment provided by "Wurm's Orchestra."[54] Although members hosted a wide variety of events and studied a diversity of subjects, Mrs. John King Ottley expressed concern over the lack of depth of their experiences. She recommended the Club explore systematic courses of study presented by professionals. She particularly recommended university extension programs with lectures on subjects such as sociology. One meeting's program focused on social ethics and included topics related to civics, international relations, and social class.[55]

Seeing the tremendous benefits of educational advancement, members of the Atlanta Woman's Club sought enlightenment not only for themselves, but also for others. Emboldened by their passion for learning, they influenced the development of educational programs, the creation of schools, and the formation of bodies of women who would influence those schools. In reaching out to the Atlanta Community, a clubwoman stated, "We are working not only for higher culture among the better educated class of women, but helping to unblock the ranks of the uneducated masses by presenting them opportunities of great value in the line of cheap lectures from America's best scholars, and by aiding in the establishment of night schools among factory children."[56]

During its early years, Atlanta Woman's Club members focused on social issues dear to their hearts. They were determined to learn about these issues and to have an impact in each area. Among their program topics were "Social Economics," "Municipalities," "Commercial Law," and "How to Deal with Poverty, Crime, and Disease."[57]

The more members learned and worked together, the more they realized the value of acquiring knowledge related to specific issues, the power of the Club's influence, and the immense possibilities that arose when their influence was unified with that of other clubs. A news article clipping in the Club scrapbook summed it up: "The Atlanta Woman's Club is realizing its responsibility as well as its power in the influence that it can exert along with other organizations of women, over industrial conditions as they affect women and children. They can influence both public sentiment and legislation, but first, they must know the evils as they exist. To know will be to sympathize; then comes the desire to help; and half the battle is won. For nothing can stand against the full tide of woman's will and wish. That is where the beauty of organization comes in. One woman may be a power. A thousand women are sure to be."[58]

Club members wanted a public kindergarten, better working conditions and more political and legal rights for women, and child labor laws. Their concerns reflected local needs and, eventually, issues of interest to other Georgia clubs and those in the subsequent Georgia Federation (GaFWC) and the General Federation (GFWC). One of their ongoing goals was to alleviate the bleak lives of the lower class, which they referred to as the "submerged world." In working with the latter, the women urged one-on-one contact as part of their effort's success.[59]

In reaching out to mothers and their children, the Club set up classes related to childcare and provided educational materials such as globes, pictures, and books to local schools. Volumes and volumes of books were collected for traveling libraries destined to reach rural areas.[60] The women remained adamant in rejecting identification with suffragettes (whom they pictured as unfeminine), but they supported the welfare and protection of children in every condition of life, including home, school, and factories, as well as all that developed and elevated women, mentally, spiritually, and socially. As the years passed, they became increasingly concerned for women and children who were geographically isolated from the mainstream, such as those in Georgia's mountainous areas.[61]

From its beginning, the Atlanta Woman's Club joined others in advocating support of both urban and rural communities through the purchase of homegrown, homemade Georgia products. In the early years of the Club, Mrs. Charles Cook, Mrs. Henry Grady, and Mrs. Frances Gordon Smith were appointed to the Club's finance committee. Among their first actions was the urging of the wearing of white cotton stockings in order to increase sales of that product and help Georgia farmers. Later, the Club was among the state's leaders in the movement to diversify and introduce new crops, thereby increasing agricultural profits.[62]

Members continued to collect initiation fees and dues to help finance the Club and its projects, and they also launched many fundraising activities. Many members were convinced that the Atlanta Woman's Club, and other women, should be as busi-

57 "Club Women Heartily Second the Move." Unidentified newspaper clipping, 1895 scrapbook, *Atlanta Woman's Club Scrapbook Collection*, MSS 326–60.

58 Unidentified newspaper clipping, 1895 scrapbook, *Atlanta Woman's Club Scrapbook Collection*, MSS 326–60.

59 General information throughout 1895 scrapbook, *Atlanta Woman's Club Scrapbook Collection*, MSS 326–60; "Educating Mothers Is as Important as Teaching Children," 13 Apr 1897, unidentified newspaper clipping, 1895 scrapbook, *Atlanta Woman's Club Scrapbook Collection*, MSS 326–60.

60 Notes and unidentified articles, 1895 scrapbook, *Atlanta Woman's Club Scrapbook Collection*, MSS 326–60.

61 "Georgia Club Women Abolish Silk Petticoats?" unidentified clipping, 1895 scrapbook, *Atlanta Woman's Club Scrapbook Collection*, MSS 326-60.

62 Biennial Report, Atlanta Woman's Club, 1944–1946, p. 62, MSS 353, Kenan Research Center; notes and clippings from 1895 scrapbook, *Atlanta Woman's Club Scrapbook Collection*; "Women are a Unit for the Textile Education of Girls," *The Atlanta Constitution*, Sept 1898, 1895 scrapbook, *Atlanta Woman's Club Scrapbook Collection*, MSS 326–60.

63 "Club Women Heartily Second the Move," unidentified newspaper clipping, 1895 scrapbook, *Atlanta Woman's Club Scrapbook Collection*, MSS 326–60.

64 Notes, 1895 scrapbook, *Atlanta Woman's Club Scrapbook Collection*, MSS 326–60; King, Mrs. William, "The Highest Type of Life and the Effects of Club Life on Women," address at Monteagle TN on Federation Day, Atlanta Woman's Club scrapbook #1, p. 59, Atlanta History Center, Atlanta GA, MSS 326-60/.

65 Notes, no date, 1895 scrapbook, *Atlanta Woman's Club Scrapbook Collection*, MSS 326–60.

66 Notes and clippings, 1895 scrapbook, *Atlanta Woman's Club Scrapbook Collection*, MSS 326–60.

67 "Mrs. Nellie Peters Black on the Reform Movement," unidentified newspaper clipping from 1897, in 1895 scrapbook, *Atlanta Woman's Club Scrapbook Collection*, MSS 326–60.

ness-minded as themselves. According to Mrs. John King Ottley, "No Atlanta Club woman will expect her checks to be honored so long as her checkbook holds out."[63]

The clubwomen tended to be powerful, influential, and wealthy, but believing that no otherwise desirable woman who sought membership but lacked financial means should be excluded, the women supplemented their income by attaching a large board to the clubroom wall and selling advertising space to local merchants. Merchants purchased their ads in 1-foot-square increments at the rate of $10 per year. Among those seeking to advertise on the board were businesses such as a "butcher, baker, candlestick maker, a dry goods store, jeweler, carriage maker, blacksmith and picture-framer."[64] Within short order, local businesses realized the women were not only posting information about them, but also were patronizing them. Urging their colleagues to follow suit, the women advocated shopping at home from supported businesses rather than ordering from outside the city. Woe be to the merchants who did not purchase ads![65]

Clubwomen also demonstrated financial finesse by procuring lecturers for club programs and "lending" them for a price to organizations in other areas. One example was Professor Dunn, an instructor of Ethnology from the University of Cincinnati, who taught a six-week course on "The Peoples of Europe." By arranging a circuit of tours that included Knoxville, Rome, Macon, and Barnesville, the Club made $250. The women's knowledge expanded, and so did their interests. Areas of exploration included topics related to physiology, psychology, body language, literature and the arts, history, sociology, heredity versus environment, taxation, religion, political science, law, and current events.[66]

At the same time that the Atlanta Woman's Club was fostering business and education principles in its members and in the community, society as a whole was questioning the feasibility of trying to educate women. Current cultural norms put no faith in women's strength and abilities yet held them accountable and responsible for their families' and their communities' wellbeing. In cases of failure, women were burdened with an overwhelming sense of guilt.

In 1897, Nellie Peters Black, chairman of the Reform Committee, addressed the Atlanta Woman's Club on the reform movement and women's state of affairs: "I don't know if it has ever occurred to you, my sisters, to go back beyond the days of our grandmothers, those good old ladies whose domestic virtues are always being held up before the women of today, back beyond their spinning wheels and knitting needles, down through long shadowy paths of generation after generation of women, until we reach the very first woman of all, Eve in the Garden of Eden. Here, woman as a reformer first asserted her sway; it was Eve who desired more knowledge, she first suggested plucking the fruit from the tree of knowledge, and Adam, manlike, laid the blame of the disobedience upon 'the woman thou gavest me.' Then, as now, poor woman must bear the blame of a failure; when success comes, a man is always near to wear the honor."[67]

In *Loosening Corsets*, A. Louise Staman notes that to many, a woman's knowledge of science, history, Greek, and politics was not just irrelevant; it was dangerous and contrary to the smooth running of her home. Well-known scientists of the day contended that strenuous education, particularly higher education, could damage a woman's nervous system and her physical wellbeing. In *Sex and Education*, former Harvard Medical School professor Dr. Edward H. Clarke asserted, "Women who went to college were likely to suffer mental and physical breakdowns and possible sterility. Women as a whole were deemed inferior and highly educated women less charming."[68] Despite these beliefs, the Atlanta Woman's Club was undaunted. One member aptly appraised the situation: "It is not what has been done to woman, so much as what has been made of her."[69]

[68] Staman, *Loosening Corsets* (Macon GA: Tiger Iron Press, 2006) 122–23.

[69] "Whence? Wherefore? Whither?" unidentified article containing excerpts from Mrs. J. K. Ottley's address at the General Federation Convention in Monteagle TN, 1897, in 1895 scrapbook, *Atlanta Woman's Club Scrapbook Collection*, MSS 326–60.

CHAPTER SIX

At the polls, infants, imbeciles and women are not allowed to vote.
State universities, no women allowed. Workers Wanted: No women
need apply. Professional field—Women will please keep off the grass.

Anonymous GaFWC Clubwoman, 1900[70]

The Atlanta Woman's Club was quickly recognized by Northern clubs as a power in the South and a leader in organizing Southern women. The Club had been active less than a year when members decided to expand its reach and purpose as a force for good on a local level. In 1896, AWC members joined with the Sorosis Club in Elberton, Georgia, in pushing to establish a Georgia Federation of Women's Clubs. The two clubs were considered the most prominent in the state.

From 27 through 29 October 1896, the clubs hosted a three-day Atlanta conference in the hope of bringing together delegates from every woman's club in Georgia. Almost twenty clubs sent representatives, and, after two days of open forum, the Georgia Federation of Women's Clubs was chartered. In becoming the governing structure for Georgia's woman's club movement, the GaFWC brought together a diversity of clubs as a force for the good of the state. The new organization set forth an agenda to identify and address local and regional needs. Rebecca Douglas Lowe was so enthusiastic that she resigned her presidency of the Atlanta Woman's Club to become the Federation's new president.

Mrs. Lowe immediately set about to improve the conditions of rural schools and create a state library commission. With her guidance, the Federation adopted green and white as its colors, the Cherokee Rose as the Federation flower, and Georgia's state motto, "Wisdom, Justice and Moder-

71 Notes, November, 1895 scrapbook, *Atlanta Woman's Club Scrapbook Collection*, MSS 326–60, Kenan Research Center, Atlanta History Center, Atlanta GA; "Woman's Club Notes," 1895 scrapbook, *Atlanta Woman's Club Scrapbook Collection*, MSS 326–360; "For Our Mutual Benefit: The Athens Woman's Club and Social Reform, 1899–1920," no date, Athens Woman's Club collection, Heritage Room, Athens–Clarke County Library, Athens GA, Digital Library of Georgia/GALILEO (Athens GA: University of Georgia Libraries, 2006–2007), dlg.galileo.usg.edu/athenswomansclub/ (accessed 12 October 2009); "GaFWC History," GFWC/Georgia Federation of Women's Clubs, www.gafwc.org/html/gafwc_history.html

72 "GaFWC History," GFWC/Georgia Federation of Women's Clubs, www.gafwc.org/html/gafwc_history.html; Houde, *Reaching Out: A Story of the General Federation of Women's Clubs* (Washington/Chicago: Mobium Press, 1989) 77.

73 "For Our Mutual Benefit."

74 "Form," 1895 scrapbook, *Atlanta Woman's Club Scrapbook Collection*, MSS 326–60; Harlan, Smock, and Kraft, *The Booker T. Washington Papers*, vol. 5: 1899–1900 (Chicago: University of Illinois Press, 1976) 560, www.history cooperative.org/btw/vol.5/html/560.html

75 "Federation News," unidentified newspaper clipping, 1895 scrapbook, *Atlanta Woman's Club Scrapbook Collection*, MSS 326–60.

ation," as its own. Spurred by her leadership, the organization's members found themselves moving from addressing goals of individual members and clubs to working in unison for others.[71]

At this time, the state of Georgia was also addressing changes. Political and social issues focused attention on challenges related to urbanization, industrialization, education, and women's changing roles. Because of the state's regional and geographical diversity, the Industrial Age divided it into agrarian and urban societies. Two Georgias emerged, and their differences compounded Federation challenges. Mrs. Lowe led the Georgia Federation and its member clubs in working toward a better quality of life in both urban and rural areas. Among member clubs' concerns were the needs for broader educational facilities, the establishment of libraries, improved farm production, better roads, and equal rights for women.

Education was the topic of the day as women of the GaFWC and other nonaffiliated Georgia clubs reflected the national concern that little progress would be made in areas of education and reform without a competent and well-informed citizenry. At the time, Georgia had no school attendance law and provided no public libraries or books for rural children. Within a year of its organization, the Georgia Federation of Women's Clubs' Educational Committee conducted a survey of the state's educational conditions and library needs. The results were published in a brochure that covered the educational system from kindergarten to college. The publication suggested innovative reforms, which were so well received that other states included them in their educational plans.

In an effort to provide reading materials to isolated sections of the state, the women expanded their traveling library to make books and articles available to clubs that paid the costs to ship them to rural areas. To facilitate their goals, clubwomen secured the cooperation of Seaboard Air Line Railway to transport a library housed in and circulated from the home of the state chairman, Mrs. E. B. Heard. The library was available to all towns on the railroad line in South Carolina, North Carolina, and Georgia. In addition, the Atlanta Woman's Club and other individual clubs collected books for their local communities.[72]

A charismatic leader, Mrs. Lowe later became president of the General Federation of Women's Clubs, where she played an important role in selecting the types of reform the national Federation pursued. National Federation leaders hoped her election to that position would promote the growth and development of club life in the South.[73] Lowe was an avid reader and often sat on the veranda of her red brick home, surrounded by a large and well-kept lawn, attending to her correspondence or searching the Atlanta, New York, and London papers for current club work news. Her ongoing concerns included improved working conditions and wages for women and child labor issues.[74] She stated, "The time has come in our history when as women we realize that whether she comes from the walks of life where ease and luxury dwell, or whether she be a representative of the wage-earning class, the truth is still the same that, as women, we owe it to our sex to raise a voice in this land for the protection of women against want, oppression, injustice and ignorance."[75]

On the national level, the General Federation united women in common purposes while eliminating political barriers. As Georgia Federation member Isma

Dooley observed, "The club spirit now paramount among women has done more to overcome sectional prejudices between the women of the North and South than any other power since the days of the Confederacy. The club woman of the new South is as closely allied to her sister of the North as she is to one from kindred southern states."[76] The GFWC as a whole addressed national issues of reform while individual clubs became involved in local community needs and state federations worked on regional problems within individual states.

The First Annual Convention of the Georgia Federation of Women's Clubs was held in Rome, Georgia, from 2 to 4 November 1896, while Mrs. Lowe was still president.[77] According to Isma Dooley, much work was needed, but there was hope: "The educational outlook in Georgia is encouraging. While we stand near the foot in the scale of literacy, we see signs of aroused interest and awakened conscience. A knowledge of one's ignorance is the highest wisdom. Let 'No backward steps' be Georgia's motto."[78]

The GaFWC's second president was Atlanta Woman's Club member Mrs. Lindsay Johnson, who served two years. Her concerns mirrored much of those of Mrs. Lowe and the General Federation on education and the issue of children working in factories. Under her direction, the organization published a yearbook urging member clubs to work with legislators on pushing through a Child Labor Bill and a Compulsory Education Bill and selected the *Atlanta Constitution* as the Federation's official media outlet. The *Constitution* and other newspapers had a great effect on the woman's movement because the achievements of clubs were reported for all women to see. Often, many articles were consolidated in one impactful section or page. The Club also petitioned for a charter of incorporation from the state of Georgia.[79]

According to GaFWC records, in 1900, women were still barred from all state-supported institutions of higher learning. That year, the GaFWC held a state convention during which Mrs. Johnson requested that the clubwomen seek passage of legislation to prohibit children under twelve from working, to raise the age of consent to ten years old, and to allow the admission of girls in textiles studies at the Georgia Institute of Technology. A "Field Day" was also held at Warm Springs, Georgia. The 500 women present made plans for a "bigger and more forceful club life," and the event was so successful it became the forerunner of the Georgia Federation's (GaFWC) "Institute."[80]

Concerns and accomplishments of the early GaFWC included the publication of its first official periodical, *The Southern Woman*; cooperative efforts for improved farm production; better roads; equal rights for women; and a proposal to amend laws related to lunacy, evidence of their early concern with mental health issues. Additional initiatives included a proposal for the study of domestic science to be included in all schools; the suggestion that vocational training be introduced to Georgia schools; continuing requests that girls be allowed into the University of Georgia and the Textile Department of the Georgia Intstitute of Technology; a statewide exhibition of handiwork fashioned by rural-urban women; the enactment of the traveling libraries; the promotion of compulsory education; and a petition to the governor calling for "Qualifications being equal in applicant for position of State Librarian,

76 Unidentified newspaper clipping referring to a prior *Atlanta Constitution* article, "Women in These Days," 1895 scrapbook, *Atlanta Woman's Club Scrapbook Collection*, MSS 326–60.

77 First Annual Convention: "Georgia Federation of Women's Clubs Handbook," 1895 scrapbook, *Atlanta Woman's Club Scrapbook Collection*, MSS 326–60.

78 Unidentified newspaper clipping referring to "Women in These Days," MSS 326–60.

79 "GaFWC History," www.gafwc.org/html/gafwc_ history.html; notes, no date, Wimbish House Archives, Atlanta GA; interview by Anne B. Jones with A. Louise Staman, 10 Nov 2010.

80 "GaFWC History," www.gafwc.org/ html/gafwc_history.html.

81 "Library Convention Over," 1897, unidentified clipping, in 1895 scrapbook, *Atlanta Woman's Club Scrapbook Collection*, MSS 326–60; notes and unidentified articles, MSS 326–60.

82 "A Bright Report of the Past Year's Work of the Atlanta Woman's Club," unidentified article source, General Information throughout 1896–1920, *Atlanta Woman's Club Scrapbook Collection*, MSS 326–60.

83 "GaFWC History," www.gafwc.org /html/gafwc_history.html.

84 Ibid.

preference given to a woman." The organization also called for the date of 7 December to be called Arbor Day, though the reason for this is unknown.

Other ongoing issues the women were concerned with included the state's inability to coordinate educational and library services. Members of the Atlanta Woman's Club and the State Federation (GaFWC) urged the creation of a state library commission. To facilitate this goal, the AWC hosted a library convention that resulted in a state association for libraries. AWC also demonstrated its appreciation for local teachers by supporting them and honoring them with special events.[81] In 1897, Georgia's state school superintendent commented on the work of the Atlanta Woman's Club by saying that in its study of state and county school systems, the AWC had "put the whole town to thinking."[82]

The clubwomen of the Georgia Federation persistently addressed the introduction of school-based vocational training. Since no Georgians were qualified to teach these subjects, the clubwomen obtained scholarships and paid two years' expenses for the first Georgia women trained to teach home economics and manual training (a precursor to vocational training), with the agreement they should come back to teach in the state. Although it would be years before they saw the fruits of their efforts, the GaFWC's commitment to child labor reform was ongoing and members continually applied pressure on the Georgia legislature.[83]

During this time, "Equal Rights for Women was presented to the State Legislature in the following resolution: 'Females are entitled to the privilege of the elective franchise, to hold any civil office or perform any civil function in as full and complete a manner as the same can be employed by any male citizen; provided, however, females shall not be liable to discharge military, jury, police, or road duty.'"[84]

In the second decade of the twenty-first century, the Georgia Federation of Women's Clubs includes approximately 150 general, junior, or juniorette clubs with a combined membership of around 5,000. Every Georgia clubwoman is also a member of the General Federation of Women's Clubs whose focus continues to be volunteer service. Each individual Georgia club includes the following six community service programs: Arts, Conservation, Education, Home Life, International Outreach, and Public Issues.

Each member selects a community service program in which to work according to her interests. There are also special committees and other opportunities for community involvement and leadership development. The GaFWC issues an annual "call" to all clubs to attend a state institute and state convention where members network and learn from each other.

The clubs are divided into ten districts with each sponsoring its own presidents, platforms, and annual meetings. The organization's members are supportive of the state president's and international president's platforms, which are related to public issues. Recent campaigns have included prevention of coronary disease and domestic violence.

The Georgia Federation, along with other states, supports the 1734 Society, which is devoted to the enhancement and maintenance of the General Federation of Women's Clubs headquarters located at 1734 N Street NW, Washington, DC, 20036. Built in 1875, and owned by the General Federation since 1922, GFWC International

Headquarters is a National Historic Landmark. The headquarters contains the offices of the GFWC professional staff, is home to the international president during her term of office, houses the GFWC Women's History and Resource Center, provides a center for women's issues and outreach, and offers support and guidance to more than 100,000 members from more than 4000 clubs who collaborate on projects that touch lives in their hometowns, in their states, and around the globe. The Women's History and Resource Center preserves collections of materials from the GFWC and its member federations and clubs and makes them accessible through research services, exhibitions, tours, and programs. The collections are housed in a National Historic Landmark building that includes archives, a research library, and museum-quality art and artifacts. This is an important responsibility of the clubs as the headquarters is one of only 5 percent of National Historical Landmarks related to women's history. GFWC publishes the *GFWC Clubwoman Magazine* six times a year. GaFWC's official publication is the *Georgia Clubwoman*.[85]

85 "General Federation of Women's Clubs," www.gfwc.org; *Timeline Calendar 2010*, Women's History and Resource Center, General Federation of Women's Clubs, Washington DC; "1734 Society," no date, promotional brochure, General Federation of Women's Clubs.

CHAPTER SEVEN

Clubs are simply in the very nature of things; they are one of the modern manifestations of good old fashioned religion. A great wave of them is sweeping over the civilized world and just now Atlanta is one of the storm centers. Clubs are interesting; intelligent questions are brightly put and funny things happen there. Delightful little tiffs electrify the atmosphere occasionally and charming friendships are made.

Mrs. Julius L. Brown[86]

At the dawn of the twentieth century, the Atlanta Woman's Club was experiencing a period of growth, increased cooperation with other clubs, new projects, and changing administrations. During the late 1800s, Mrs. Lowe was replaced as president by Mrs. J. K. Ottley (1896–1897), followed by Mrs. Charles Reid (1897–1898), Mrs. W. P. Pattillo (1898–1899), and Mrs. Burton Smith (1899–1900). The nation was in a "Gilded Age," constantly changing with expanding technology. Mass-produced newspapers, movies, the gramophone, the telephone, and newly formed sports teams propelled the country toward a more homogeneous national culture. Combined with the advent of rural free mail delivery, some clubwomen feared these new developments would cause a decline in reading and foster an unquestioning mass culture in which emotionally charged propaganda could control the public.[87]

86 "City Federation Now Has More than 2000 Members," unidentified newspaper clipping, Scrapbook 1896–1920, Atlanta Woman's Club Scrapbook Collection, MSS 326–360, Kenan Research Center, Atlanta History Center, Atlanta GA.

87 Atlanta Woman's Club, unidentified paper, Wimbish House Archives; Houde, *Reaching Out: A Story of the General Federation of Women's Clubs* (Washington/Chicago: Mobium Press, 1989) 85; "Mass Culture," *Student's Friend World History and Geography*, p. 40, www.studentsfriend.com (24 September 2009).

88 Matthew Held, *The New Georgia Encyclopedia*, University of West Georgia, 3 November 2006.

89 Unidentified clipping, 1895 scrapbook, *Atlanta Woman's Club Scrapbook Collection*, MSS 326–60.

90 "Julius L. Brown Dead," *The New York Times*, 6 Sep 1910, Kenan Research Center; 1896–1920 *Atlanta Woman's Club Scrapbook Collection*, MSS 326–60, Kenan Research Center; unidentified clippings, Scrapbook 2, *Atlanta Woman's Club Scrapbook Collection*, MSS 326–60; Percy, Mrs. William Lewis, secretary of the City Federation, "Since Organization in March, 1899, Federation Has Done Great Work," *Atlanta Constitution*, 4 Jun 1913, Kenan Research Center.

For the first time in the history of Atlanta and the United States, women were gaining tremendous power through numbers and using it for the common good. In the late 1800s, Georgia's politics had been dominated by three of the state's most influential figures, Joseph E. Brown, General John B. Gordon, and General Alfred H. Colquitt. This so-called "Bourbon Triumvirate" had wielded enormous political weight.[88]

Members of the Atlanta Woman's Club and the Georgia Federation were well aware of their strength and the complexity of the political climate. They recognized their need for increased power yet understood their political vulnerability, which was due not only to gender, but also to the state's economic, regional, religious, and party differences. An address delivered before the State Federation of Women's Clubs warned of losing strength through political partisanship, and the AWC took note. Atlanta Woman's Club members maintained a neutral stance as they sought ways to increase their influence.[89]

By the late 1800s, Atlanta's population and its number and variety of women's clubs were increasing. Clubs were spread throughout the city, and their memberships and causes overlapped. Already aware of the potential of organized power, the Atlanta Woman's Club seized the opportunity to form inter-club alliances.

Mrs. W. P. Pattillo led the membership in applying the ideas of unity and political neutrality in organizing Atlanta's clubs into a city federation. Her idea was well received, and representatives from sixteen organizations met at her home on 28 March 1899 to form the Atlanta City Federation. Mrs. Julius Brown became the group's first president. With ties to Georgia's former governor, Joseph E. Brown, and future governor, Joseph M. Brown, Mrs. Brown indirectly had access to the most powerful politicians in Georgia.[90]

The Atlanta City Federation began at once working with the Georgia Federation of Women's Clubs to present a woman's exhibit at the upcoming State Fair. Members also worked in conjunction with the Atlanta Woman's Club and Georgia Federation on issues related to child labor, kindergartens, libraries, and juvenile justice. In 1900, a City Federation committee, including Atlanta Woman's Club member Nellie Peters Black, went before a grand

Mrs. Rebecca Douglas Lowe
Founder, 1895–1896

Mrs. J. K. Ottley
1896–1897

Mrs. Charles Reid
1897–1898

Mrs. W. P. Pattillo
1898–1899

Mrs. Burton Smith
1899–1900

jury to ask for an election to establish a juvenile reformatory. The election was called and the reformatory was established. Another accomplishment was obtaining a probation officer of the juvenile courts.[91]

After receiving invitations from Atlanta Woman's Club members Rebecca Douglas Lowe (president of GFWC) and Mrs. J. Lindsay Johnson (president of GaFWC), the Atlanta City Federation—which no longer exists—joined the Georgia and General Federations.[92] The Atlanta Woman's Club leaders and others put tremendous effort into coordinating work between the clubs while each club also worked to promote its own goals. According to Mrs. Brown, "The decline in gossip is really startling. Not so much that we are better than we used to be, but we just haven't time."[93]

The Atlanta City Federation eventually reached 8,000 members. Its accomplishments were made possible due to its nonpartisanship, its devotion to public good, and the energy of its members. The formation of the Georgia Federation and Atlanta City Federation, as well as other organizational efforts by its members, led to the Atlanta Woman's Club being referred to as the "Mother of Federation in Georgia."[94]

As the women's club movement passed into the 1900s, the Atlanta Woman's Club, the Atlanta City Federation, the Georgia Federation, and the General Federation of Women's Clubs waged unrelenting efforts to promote health and hygiene, education, conservation, libraries, child welfare, women's rights, and clubwomen's own academic and cultural improvement.

Among the topics the Atlanta Woman's Club members studied were philanthropy, "Heredity versus Environment," music, and foreign and domestic current events. Gradually, the women focused on current events as they realized their growing power and influence made them more capable of enacting change. They were becoming a viable force in local and national reform.[95]

In 1900, the Atlanta Woman's Club organized an Arts and Crafts Committee in order to give recognition "to the world-wide movement toward self-expression for every individual through the work of the hand. The greatest need along this line in Georgia lies in the promotion of the fireside crafts in which our people are so lacking."[96] The committee exhibited European and self-made crafts in the club rooms and held a pre-Christmas sale featuring handwork from all over the state that had been "here-to-fore undeveloped in Georgia, such as hand-weaving, rug making, jute embroidery, basketry and straw plaiting." The women set out to teach these crafts.[97]

Although their power and influence were expanding, the Atlanta Woman's Club and other Georgia clubwomen remained rooted in Southern conventions of

91 "Since Organization"; Johnson, Mrs. J. Lindsay, "Bills We've Lost and Won," *Atlanta Constitution*, 4 Jun 1913; unidentified clippings, Scrapbook 2, MSS 326–60.

92 Unidentified clippings, Scrapbook 2, MSS 326–60.

93 "The City Federation of Women's Clubs Meets," unidentified clipping, Scrapbook 2, MSS 326–60.

94 Mrs. Charles J. Hadin, president of the Atlanta City Federation, "Atlanta City Federation of Woman's Clubs: Foreword," *Atlanta Constitution*, 4 Jun 1913; Coles, Mrs. A.P., Atlanta Woman's Club president, "Atlanta City Federation of Woman's Clubs," *Atlanta Constitution*, 4 Jun 1913.

95 Notes, 1895 scrapbook, *Atlanta Woman's Club Scrapbook Collection*, MSS 326–60; Houde, *Reaching Out*, 79.

96 Ada Biehl, "Do You Remember?" Atlanta Woman's Club Biennial Report—1966–1968, Wimbish House Archives; Biennial Report, 1966–1968, MSS 353, Kenan Research Center.

97 Biehl, "Do You Remember?"

98 "For Our Mutual Benefit: The Athens Woman's Club and Social Reform, 1899–1920," no date, Athens Woman's Club collection, Heritage Room, Athens-Clarke County Library, Athens GA, Digital Library of Georgia/GALILEO (Athens GA: University of Georgia Libraries, 2006–2007), dlg.galileo.usg.edu/athenswomansclub (accessed 12 October 2009); "GaFWC History," GFWC/Georgia Federation of Women's Clubs, www.gafwc.org/html/gafwc_history.html.

99 Ibid.

100 Notes, Atlanta Woman's Club, Wimbish House Archives.

101 "Spanish-American War," p. 37, www.studentsfriend.com (accessed 24 September 1009).

102 Author unknown, "Is War a Necessity? Atlanta Women Answer," unidentified clipping, *Atlanta Journal*, 1895 scrapbook. Atlanta Woman's Club Scrapbooks Collection, MSS 326-60. Kenan Research Center. Atlanta History Center.

womanhood. Drawing upon that tradition, "They used their socially-prescribed positions as mothers, home-makers, and caretakers as qualifying credentials for their new public roles."[98] This tendency reflected a wider trend by which "Nineteenth century notions surrounding the ideas of womanhood and the cult of domesticity lingered throughout Georgia well into the twentieth century. Members of the Atlanta Woman's Club and other Georgia clubs capitalized on these ideas, assimilating them into their movement rhetoric by coining terms such as 'social mothering' and 'municipal housekeeping' to describe their civic and municipal reform endeavors."[99]

Leading the Atlanta Woman's Club into these years was Mrs. E. G. McCabe (1900–1901), Mrs. James Jackson (1901–1902), and Mrs. Edward Brown (1902–1904).[100] During the early years of the new century, the United States was expanding its manifest destiny to lands overseas. Siding with Cuban rebels who were fighting for their independence, the US made a show of support and power by sending the battleship *Maine* to Havana's harbor. When the ship exploded, killing 266 American sailors, the US mistakenly blamed Spain and declared war. The Spanish-American War lasted only four months but destroyed Spain's power in the West and its standing in the world.[101]

The United States was victorious, but Atlanta women had mixed feelings about war. Seeing an opportunity to address a controversial issue, the *Atlanta Journal* encouraged them to give opinions on whether war was a necessity. Among those responding was Atlanta Woman's Club member Rebecca Douglas Lowe. Stating, "War never leaves a nation where it found it," she submitted that in light of the present, war might be necessary, but she nonetheless looked to women's influence to hasten the day when wrongs would be adjusted without force. She saw the United States' expansion, imperialism, prosperity, and violation of other nations' boundaries as actions that fostered bitterness.

A visionary, Lowe foresaw that the influence of wise, conservative, peace-loving women would profoundly affect the future. This influence, she felt, when united with the "powers that be," could aid in establishing a tribunal that would represent all nations and redress wrongs through arbitration, not war.[102]

Mrs. E. G. McCabe
1900–1901

Mrs. James Jackson
1901–1902

Mrs. Edward T. Brown
1902–1904

CHAPTER EIGHT

So long as children six years of age are employed in mills and factories in any part of the United States and there is the crying need for uniform laws regarding child labor . . . can (any club) say it has no responsibility. . . ?

GFWC Board of Directors[103]

The world of Atlanta Woman's Club members was rapidly changing as Georgia entered a period of economic growth and resource development. At the turn of the twentieth century, Atlanta had become the "hub of the regional economy," and its swelling population put a strain on municipal services.[104] Residents living outside of Atlanta were also facing challenges. Despite the growing popularity of automobiles and improved communication, much of the population generally remained on farms and led isolated, subsistence lives. Tenant farmers and sharecroppers lived a poverty-ridden existence, often struggling to survive. Workers pulled to Atlanta by the Industrial Revolution and urbanization longed for the good old days when the farm provided not only fresh produce, but also a sense of community.[105]

Recognizing this need, Atlanta Woman's Club president Mrs. Burton Smith formed a committee to look into the ways and means of sponsoring a city market. Members were asked to secure names and addresses of truck farmers (those willing to bring their produce to the city to sell) and poultry raisers in and around Atlanta and to ask those who supported a local farmer's market to sign a petition to the city council. The plan was to have

103 Houde, *Reaching Out: A Story of the General Federation of Women's Clubs* (Washington/Chicago: Mobium Press, 1989) 93. Quote is from the early twentieth century.

104 "Atlanta Race Riot of 1906," *History & Archaeology*, www.georgiaencyclopedia.org/nge/Article.jsp?id= h-3033 (accessed 4 March 2010).

105 Project for Public Spaces, "Sweet Auburn Curb Market," *Great Public Spaces*, www.pps.org/great_ public_spaces/one?public_place_id=182 (accessed 29 December 2009).

106 Atlanta Woman's Club Handbook 1899–1900, 1895 scrapbook, *Atlanta Woman's Club Scrapbook Collection*, MSS 326–60, Kenan Research Center, Atlanta History Center, Atlanta GA.

107 Houde, *Reaching Out*, 89.

108 Houde, *Reaching Out*, 95.

109 "Timeline," Women's History and Resource Center, General Federation of Women's Clubs, Washington DC.

110 "For Our Mutual Benefit: The Athens Woman's Club and Social Reform, 1899–1920," no date, Athens Woman's Club collection, Heritage Room, Athens-Clarke County Library, Athens GA, Digital Library of Georgia/GALILEO (Athens GA: University of Georgia Libraries, 2006–2007), dlg.galileo.usg.edu/athenswomansclub (accessed 12 October 2009); Houde, *Reaching Out*, 96–97.

111 Dinah Peevy, "Mary Ann Lipscomb," unpublished research paper, 2009, presented spring 2010 at Atlanta Woman's Club meeting.

112 "For Our Mutual Benefit"; Houde, *Reaching Out*, 96–97; Peevy, "Mary Ann Lipscomb."

Atlanta housewives also sign this petition expressing the need for the market and asking for a portion of a street to be allocated for its use. Farmers, gardeners, poultry-raisers and butchers could sell their goods during specified hours each day. The women hoped to gain public support and, eventually, a permanent building to house the produce.[106]

One stubborn issue the Georgia Federation and other reform-oriented organizations found slow to change was the unrelenting practice of child labor. In addressing the problem, the General Federation's 1898 convention in Denver, Colorado, had prompted a resolution ". . . that no child under 14 years of age be employed in mill, factory, workshop, store, office, or laundry, and no boy under 16 years of age employed in mines. . . ; that adequate school facilities, including manual training, be provided for every child up to the age of 14 years and that laws be enforced. . . ; that in mill, factory, workshop, laundry, and mercantile establishment, the maximum working day for women and children shall not exceed eight hours or 48 hours per week. . . ; that each club appoint a standing committee to inquire into labor conditions. . . ; that each state federation appoint a similar committee to investigate state labor laws and those relating to sanitation and protection for women and children." Despite this resolution, for years, child labor remained an ongoing challenge for the General Federation, Georgia Federation, and Atlanta Woman's Club.[107]

As GFWC president, Atlanta Woman's Club member Rebecca Douglas Lowe had proposed a study of factory conditions and emphasized the importance of gathering information prior to action.[108] In 1901, Chicago clubwoman and reformer Jane Addams led the General Federation of Women's Clubs' Child Labor Committee in advocating for legislation restricting child labor.[109] In 1902, former Atlanta Woman's Club member and Athens Woman's Club founder Mary Ann Lipscomb addressed the Georgia Federation, where she reported on "the alarming number of children employed in Georgia's mills and factories, and the illiteracy rates among these young people."[110]

According to current researcher and contemporary Atlanta Woman's Club member Dinah Peevy, "Mrs. Lipscomb was fearless as she faced off with the Georgia Industrial Association, Georgia's most powerful organization of mill owners, when she attempted to liberate children as young as six years of age from working in hazardous mills."[111] Enduring tremendous opposition to reform, the Atlanta Woman's Club and other Georgia Federation clubwomen attempted to circumvent the child labor question through their promotion of the compulsory education bill, the free kindergarten movement, and the promotion of educational opportunities. By 1905, Georgia clubwomen were promoting a specific child labor action program.[112]

Along with continuing their advocacy for children in the areas of child labor reform on the national level, members of the General Federation pushed for education, juvenile justice, and a juvenile court law. Atlanta Woman's Club member Nellie Peters Black was one of the most prominent Southern child advocates. Carrying on her mother's legacy of philanthropic volunteerism, she was instrumental in helping the Holy Innocence Mission of the Episcopal Church, the first denominational mission founded in Atlanta; organizing King's Daughters' Hospital, the first free hospital in Atlanta; and the founding of Grady Hospital. She served as president of the Atlanta Free Kindergarten Association and was responsible for opening several kindergartens to serve preschool children. Her work and determination influenced others to follow suit. The club supported the kindergarten movement by providing financial support and refreshments for private kindergartens in the early years and promoted their incorporation into the Atlanta public school system. Atlanta's public kindergartens owe a great debt to the Atlanta Woman's Club members of this era.[113]

Mrs. Robert Zahner
1904–1906

Mrs. A. McDouglas Wilson
1906–1908

Despite their hard-won successes, Atlanta Woman's Club members and other clubwomen throughout the General Federation recognized the challenges to public education, particularly in developing projects for their state's rural residents. Among their major concerns was the shortage of schools in isolated areas. The tenant farmers and sharecroppers of Georgia's hills and flatlands suffered from a tremendous lack of resources, and, for those in the mountainous areas, times could not be worse. Members worked to improve educational resources and opportunities by providing scholarships and promoting the consolidation of schools, the improvement of school facilities, and better pay for teachers.[114]

Taking matters into their own hands, Georgia Federation members resolved to set up several model and industrial training schools throughout the state. They raised funds, secured the land, supervised the schools' construction and furnishing, and made sure they were provided with highly trained teachers. When everything was running smoothly, they gradually relinquished control to local counties.[115] As Atlanta Woman's Club members moved forward in fostering children's rights and education, their officers tapped their talents and resources for leadership, donations, and volunteerism. Presidents during this time were Mrs. Robert Zahner (1904–1906) and Mrs. A. McDouglas Wilson (1906–1908).

113 "Mrs. Nellie Peters Black," *Women of Georgia* (Atlanta: Georgia Press Reference Association, 1927) 7; "A Brief History of Holy Innocents' Church," www.holyinnocents.org/history (accessed 10 January 2010); "For Our Mutual Benefit"; "The Atlanta Woman's Club Celebrates 100 Years," *Northside Neighbor*; Atlanta Woman's Club 1, Wimbish House Archives.

114 Houde, *Reaching Out*, 147–48; "For Our Mutual Benefit."

115 "For Our Mutual Benefit."

CHAPTER NINE

My sisters, the question for you is not what you are going to get out of the world, but what you are going to give the world.

Mary Ann Lipscomb[116]
President, Georgia Federation of Women's Clubs, 1906

thens Woman's Club member Mary Ann Lipscomb was a woman of tremendous intellect who was dedicated to freeing Georgia children from commercial labor and making their education her priority. In 1903, while vacationing in the rural mountainous region of North Georgia, she discovered that most of the area's children could not read. Classes were available only three months a year in a small, unheated room above a jail. Turning her concern into action, Mrs. Lipscomb taught reading to an assortment of mountain children on the porch of her "Cherokee Cottage." Realizing the area was in dire need of educational opportunities, she invited local citizens and summer residents to discuss the establishment of a local school. When she brought the issue before her Athens Woman's Club, members immediately began raising funds.

In 1906, while serving as the Georgia Federation of Women's Clubs president, she spoke at the organization's West Point Convention, where she made a passionate plea for help for the children and, with the Athens Woman's Club's support, offered a resolution for the Federation to establish Tallulah Falls School. The resolution passed, and the Athens Woman's Club members turned their earnings over to the Georgia Federation of Women's Clubs, which in turn began soliciting funds throughout the state. When Miss Sara White, the daughter of one of Tallulah Falls' large landholders,

---

116 Notes from papers in collection in Atlanta Wimbish House Archives; "For Our Mutual Benefit: The Athens Woman's Club and Social Reform, 1899–1920," Athen's Woman's Club Collection, Heritage Room, Athens-Clarke County Library, Athens GA, dlg.galileo.usg.edu/athenswomansclub (accessed 12 October 2009).

117 Hancock, *Not By Magic, But By Faith, Courage, and Earnest Work* (Toccoa GA: Commercial Printing Company, 1982) 11–15; Dinah Peevy, "Mary Ann Lipscomb," unpublished research paper, 2009, presented spring 2010 at Atlanta Woman's Club meeting; "For Our Mutual Benefit: The Athens Woman's Club and Social Reform, 1899–1920," no date, Athens Woman's Club collection, Heritage Room, Athens-Clarke County Library, Athens GA, Digital Library of Georgia/GALILEO (Athens GA: University of Georgia Libraries, 2006–2007), dlg.galileo.usg.edu/ athenswomansclub (accessed 12 October 2009); "Celebrating 100 Years of Tallulah Falls School," *Tallulah Falls School Magazine* 30/3 (Fall 2008): 14–19; "GaFWC History," GFWC/Georgia Federation of Women's Clubs, www.gafwc.org/html/gafwc_history. html; Hancock, *Light in the Mountains*, 15–16.

118 Mrs. Clyde F. Anderson, ed., "A Walk through History—Georgia Federation of Women's Clubs 1896–1986," paper, Wimbish House Archives, Atlanta GA.

119 Hancock, *Light in the Mountains*, 15–16.

120 "Celebrating 100 Years of Tallulah Falls School," 14–19;

121 "GaFWC History;" "History," Student Aid Foundation, Inc., http:www.studentaidfoundation.org/hist ory.html.

learned of the project, she donated 5 acres and construction began. The Atlanta Woman's Club soon became one of the school's strongest supporters.

The school's original plans included a one-story structure housing a large assembly room, two recitation rooms, a cooking room and a workshop, and large front and side porches. Upon completion, the Federation sought to provide equipment and hire qualified teachers. When a trustee position was offered to anyone donating $100 or more, Atlanta Woman's Club member Mrs. John Ottley was among the first to contribute.[117]

Tallulah Falls Industrial School was dedicated on 30 June 1909 and opened its doors on 12 July, with twenty-two students, one teacher, and Mary Ann Lipscomb serving as director. Enrollment rapidly increased and an assistant teacher was hired. Serving as a beacon of hope for the children, the school became known as "The Light in the Mountains." That same year, Georgia Federation members promoted the "very first Girls' Canning Clubs." The clubs spurred Georgia's 4-H Club movement, which has served thousands of Georgia children and is still going strong today.[118]

Travel to and from the new school was usually by foot, horseback, or railroad. Because the majority of its students lived in primitive cabins deep in the hills, they endured harsh weather and the wilds to attend, and club members were concerned. In March 1910, the teachers and two children moved into a small rental cottage furnished by the Atlanta Woman's Club. Seeing the desperate need for residential facilities, Federation members approved the building of on-campus housing. The next year, the Lipscomb Cottage was completed, at a cost of $1,500, to house teachers and students.[119]

By 1912, the school boasted two buildings, three teachers, and eighty-six students, seventeen of whom were living in the Lipscomb Cottage. In 1914, Mrs. Lipscomb's health was failing, and she turned the school's directorship over to former GaFWC president Mrs. Hugh Willet. Mrs. Willet asked that a school co-chairman be appointed in each Federation club. Four years later, Mrs. Lipscomb died. Described by the *Atlanta Constitution* as "one of the most distinguished women in the educational and social life of the south," she left a legacy of educational advocacy and action for Georgia's children. Years later, she was given the prestigious honor of being named by Georgia Women of Achievement as one of three Georgia "Women of Achievement" in 2010.[120]

Rural children were not the only group the clubs targeted for educational action. In 1908, a group of Atlanta Woman's Club members met with other Atlanta women to discuss problems facing ladies needing help to continue their adult education. The suggestion was made for the Georgia Federation to take on the project. The resulting Student Aid Foundation was the first educational foundation to be sponsored by a state federation and became a model for similar organizations throughout America. In 1950, the relationship between the GaFWC and the Student Aid Foundation was dissolved, but the foundation's work continues today. It has now served over 5,000 women.[121]

In another effort, the Georgia Federation of Women's Clubs petitioned the Georgia General Assembly to appropriate money to teach the subjects of Domestic Science and Hygiene to women at the State College of Agriculture. These efforts resulted in the Household Extension Bill. Later, member clubs paid the salaries of so-called Canning Club Agents, who eventually became the state's first Home Demonstration Agents. The organization also continued to advocate the increasing of teachers' salaries.[122]

Formal education was only one area to which Atlanta Woman's Club and Georgia Federation members devoted time. Members were appalled by the lack of knowledge and resources related to general health and hygiene. In the late 1800s, General Federation members had resolved to petition Congress to form a National Health Bureau and, in 1904, clubwoman Alice Lakey of New Jersey initiated a letter-writing campaign for pure food legislation. The GFWC took on her cause and promoted a nationwide outreach program. With health and sanitation issues a major concern of the General Federation, Georgia Federation, and the Atlanta Woman's Club, members presented numerous programs within and outside the Club to educate members and the general public.[123]

In Atlanta during these early years of the twentieth century, health facilities were limited and conditions were unsanitary. According to Athens Woman's Club records, "Cities and towns throughout Georgia were fraught with inadequate mechanisms for sewage and waste disposal, tainted water supplies, and overcrowding. Coupled with the heat and humidity of the Southern climate, these conditions provided a fertile breeding ground for communicable diseases such as cholera, malaria, typhoid fever and tuberculosis." Tuberculosis was one of the most dreaded diseases in the United States and the leading cause of death in all age groups.[124]

In 1911, Atlanta Woman's Club members advocated the passage of a city ordinance to insure the sanitary handling of foodstuffs. Along with other reformers, the clubwomen helped form the foundation of a public health movement that eventually resulted in improved sanitation, awareness, resources, and legislation. Another accomplishment of Georgia women was the passage of the Ellis Bill, which provided for the mandatory recording of the state's vital statistics.[125]

On the national level, Dr. Harvey W. Wiley, the first chief of the Pure Food Bureau, praised the General Federation of Women's Clubs as a whole, giving members a large share of credit for the Pure Food Bill's passage in 1906. In a 1911 speech, he stated, "The passage of the bill was due to the women's federated clubs of the country. Trust them to put the ball over the goal line every time. The enactment has proven the finest example of political education I have ever seen."[126] In 1912, President William H. Taft appointed Chicago clubwoman Julia Lathrop as chief of the nation's new Children's Bureau, affording GFWC members an expanded opportunity to promote public healthcare for mothers and infants, which, in turn, led to the Sheppard-Towner Act of 1921, ground-breaking legislation that funded maternity and infant healthcare.[127]

At this time, Atlanta Woman's Club leaders faced the growing need for a permanent headquarters. By 1909, the Club's building fund had reached $600. Longing for a home of their own, the members bought the old Christian Science building on Baker Street, a small white domed structure with a classical Greek façade, at a cost of $12,000. Adding $8,000 borrowed from an insurance company in Philadelphia, the Club raised the remainder of the money needed through individual

[122] Anderson, ed., A Walk through History: Georgia Federation of Women's Clubs 1896-1986. Paper, Wimbish House Archives.

[123] Houde, *Reaching Out: A Story of the General Federation of Women's Clubs* (Washington/Chicago: Mobium Press, 1989) 88. "Timeline 2010," Women's History and Resource Center, General Federation of Women's Clubs, Washington DC; Notes, 1895 scrapbook, *Atlanta Woman's Club Scrapbook Collection*, MSS 326–60, Kenan Research Center, Atlanta History Center, Atlanta GA; "For Our Mutual Benefit"; Houde, *Reaching Out*, 130.

[124] Houde, "Reaching Out," 130; "Atlanta Women Fight to Get Clean Food Law," unidentified newspaper article, Wimbish House Archives.

[125] *Atlanta Woman's Club Scrapbook, 1896–1920*, Atlanta Woman's Club Scrapbook Collection, MSS 326–60, Kenan Research Center, Atlanta History Center; "For Our Mutual Benefit"; Houde, *Reaching Out*, 131–32.

[126] "Timeline 2010."

[127] Mrs. Curtis H. Bryant, "History of the Atlanta Woman's Club," typed notes, Atlanta Woman's Club Archives.

128 Ann Taylor Boutwell, "The Grand Old Lady," unidentified article copy, Atlanta Woman's Club Archives; "History of the Atlanta Woman's Club: Its Growth and Resultful Achievements," *Atlanta Woman's Club Souvenir Book*, pp. 3–7, Wimbish House Archives; Houde, "Reaching Out," 133.

129 Houde, *Reaching Out*, 149.

130 Mrs. Z. D. Fitzpatrick, "Why Our Endowment," *Atlanta Constitution*, 4 June 1913, Wimbish House Archives.

131 Ibid.

subscriptions. Handling these challenges were presidents Mrs. Bolling Jones (1908–1909) and Mrs. Hamilton Douglas (1909–1911). The Club would remain on Baker Street for the next twelve years while the women continued to push for improvements in education, social reform, conservation, and Tallulah Falls School.[128]

This period was a time of rapid growth, not only for Georgia clubs, but also for the General Federation. The organization had become so large and diverse that its cost of operation was an overriding concern. To make sure the successful and highly praised work of the GFWC would continue, and to place the GFWC on a "permanent and efficient basis," leaders established the Sarah Platt Decker Memorial Fund.[129] The endowment plan was so favorably received many states began to develop their own endowment funds to meet member clubs' increasing financial demands. Among them were members of the Georgia Federation of Women's Clubs, including the AWC. The greatest obstacle to accomplishing their goals had always been capital, and the solution was to have a permanent source.[130]

Under the direction of then-president Ella F. White, the Georgia Federation began preliminary groundwork for an endowment fund large enough to insure a strong steady income with which the state federation could do its work and carry out its plans more effectively. After Mrs. White's untimely death while visiting an Augusta club, the fund was named in her memory.

Mrs. Bolling Jones
1908–1909

Mrs. Hamilton Douglas
1909–1911

The original charter for the Ella F. White Memorial Endowment Fund was set for a period of twenty years. It was made permanent in 1935 by action of the GaFWC Executive Board, with the First National Bank of Atlanta named as financial custodian and administrator. In 1985, Merrill, Lynch, Pierce, Fenner & Smith of Atlanta was named as the fund's financial agent. Each year, 2 percent of the net dues to the Georgia Federation of Women's Clubs are combined with contributions by clubs and individuals to add additional revenue to the fund. The Ella White Memorial Endowment Fund is under direction of five trustees nominated and elected by the GaFWC Executive Committee and ratified by the GaFWC Board. The GaFWC president, first vice president/president-elect, and director of junior clubs serve as ex-officio members of the committee. The Atlanta Woman's Club remains one of the largest contributors to the fund, which provides a significant contribution to the work of Tallulah Falls School.[131]

CHAPTER TEN

No group has been more ridiculed and caricatured than club-women, yet no group has contributed more vitality and variety to the cultural scene in this country. They have rushed in where no angel would dare put foot or wing. They have prodded and pushed men into action for civic causes from the wilderness community to the metropolitan.

Evelyn Oppenheimer[132]

n the second decade of the 1900s, the Atlanta Woman's Club became increasingly concerned about drug abuse and juvenile justice. The Club campaigned against drugs, reporting to the police "a druggist who sold morphine hypodermics for 10 cents." They worked with prisoners in both the city stockade and women's jail and assisted them upon their release. Clubwomen campaigned against the exploitation of minors and "white slave traffic" and played a role in the separation of boys from men in the city jail. Other accomplishments included establishing a chair of Domestic Science in city grammar schools and raising funds for the Industrial Home for the Blind.[133]

The efforts of the Georgia Federation and other women's organizations of this period were so astonishing that the *New York Times* commended Georgia women "for their ability to work quietly behind the scenes in getting their men-folk to bring about social reforms [such as ending the evil system of leasing convicts]."[134]

132 Wells, *Unity in Diversity*, vol. 2 of 2 (Washington DC: General Federation of Women's Clubs, 1975) 3.

133 "The Atlanta Woman's Club Celebrates 100 Years," *Northside Neighbor*, Atlanta Woman's Club History #1, Wimbish House Archives, Atlanta GA.

134 Mrs. Clyde F. Anderson, ed., "A Walk through History—Georgia Federation of Women's Clubs 1896–1986," paper, Wimbish House Archives, Atlanta GA.

135 Mrs. J. Lindsay Johnson, "Bills We've Lost and Won," *Atlanta Constitution*, 4 June 1913, Wimbish House Archives.

136 Miscellaneous notes, pp. 58–59, Atlanta Woman's Club Archives, Atlanta Woman's Club, Atlanta GA.

137 "For Our Mutual Benefit: The Athens Woman's Club and Social Reform, 1899–1920," no date, Athens Woman's Club collection, Heritage Room, Athens-Clarke County Library, Athens GA, Digital Library of Georgia/GALILEO (Athens GA: University of Georgia Libraries, 2006–2007), dlg.galileo.usg.edu/athenswomansclub (accessed 12 October 2009); 1896–1920 scrapbook, Atlanta Woman's Club Scrapbook Collection, MSS 326–60, Kenan Research Center, Atlanta History Center, Atlanta GA; Houde, *Reaching Out: A Story of the General Federation of Women's Clubs* (Washington/Chicago: Mobium Press, 1989) 137.

During the next few years the women continued their advocacy. They pushed for old and new issues, including legislation to make mothers eligible to be joint guardians with fathers in the person and property of the child, to make women eligible to serve as county school commissioners, to permit the admission of women to the state university and the textile department of the school of technology, to increase the "age of consent" of Georgia girls to twelve years, to add $1,800 for two years to the appropriation of the Demonstration Department of the State Agricultural School for courses in Domestic Science, and to provide for an appropriation in the state sufficient to build infirmaries at state institutions.[135]

According to Wimbish House Archives records, "The Atlanta Woman's Club was the first club in the State Federation to create a Good Roads Committee, an Agricultural Committee, a Committee formed for the purpose of exploiting the mineral resources of Georgia, a Committee working toward the establishment of a municipal employment bureau for the City of Atlanta, and a Committee whose duty it was to censor moving pictures for children. The first meeting of the Good Roads Congress, which was held in Atlanta, in November of 1914, was at the Atlanta Woman's Club; said meeting was held under the auspices of the Club."[136]

Another pressing issue for Atlanta clubwomen during the second decade of the twentieth century was the promotion of peace. Many had witnessed the devastation after the Civil War and other conflicts. Seeing increasing unrest among nations, they joined other American reformers who supported efforts for conflict resolution at home and abroad. As tension and conflict caused by European nationalism and imperialism escalated, concerned Americans formed peace societies devoted to diplomacy. The General Federation promoted peace through interactions with those involved in government and through peace chairmen in state federations. Generally excluded from male peace organizations, clubwomen established their own Peace Departments with educational programs.[137]

In 1914, the Georgia State Federation of Clubs for International Peace announced that the Atlanta Woman's Club would observe Peace Day on May 18, a day selected in commemoration of the first Hague Conference. All Atlanta clubs, patriotic organizations, and friends were invited to cooperate in making the day a notable occasion.

The Atlanta Woman's Club was the first club in the South to observe Peace Day and, in honor of the event, Bishop Nelson of the Episcopal Diocese of Georgia presented a program entitled "The Progress of the Peace Movement." During the meeting, members of the audience were urged to ally themselves with the worldwide community and support its great movements.

Peace chairmen were working in more than half of the GFWC state federations when the world seemed to explode. Conflict erupted in the Balkans in August 1914 when a Serbian nationalist assassinated Archduke Francis Ferdinand, Austria's heir to the throne. Austria declared war on Serbia, and Russia, Serbia's ally, declared war on Austria. Allies on both sides jumped in, spreading war like wildfire throughout Europe.

In 1915, concerned about the growing crisis, the Atlanta Woman's Club presented a program based on a dramatic reading of the "Problems of Peace and

War" (Grotius Society). Following the lead of President Woodrow Wilson, the Club remained absolutely neutral regarding the conflict in Europe. Although the meeting offered the opportunity for questions and discussion, attendees were forewarned against promoting partisanship for any belligerent nation: "The great point under discussion is what part the people of today can play in the making of a future that shall relegate war to the past, and shall work for the establishment of international harmony."[138]

President Wilson's attempt to maintain United States neutrality came to an abrupt end with the sinking of the British passenger ship *Lusitania* by a German submarine. In 1917 the United States was forced into the war by an infuriated public and economic concerns. The clubwomen immediately changed their focus from peace to war relief. That year, the Atlanta Woman's Club held a "Patriotic Day" in place of their planned peace program, began selling and purchasing Liberty Bonds, and held numerous fundraisers.

Clubwomen worked to improve the conditions of American soldiers abroad by preparing medical kits and collecting supplies such as clothing, books, and paper. Later, they were active in pushing the sales of defense bonds. They also raised money for the General Federation to give to the War Victory Commission for overseas libraries, recreation centers, and medical dispensaries. Throughout Georgia, women's clubs participated in the sponsorship and adoption of orphaned French children and provided assistance for soldiers stationed at home in army camps. Many contributed every tenth jar of their summer preserves, jellies, and canned goods to base hospitals, where they also equipped libraries.[139]

Atlanta Woman's Club projects included sponsoring a series of concerts at Fort McPherson and stocking the base's reading room. They planned entertainment for soldiers at Camp Gordon, provided the camp with magazines, gathered Christmas gifts for soldiers, sold Red Cross Christmas Seals, and organized a Red Cross Auxiliary. The women, dressed in Red Cross uniforms, raised money by selling Georgia State Automobile Association touring books at the Lakewood race track.[140]

Atlanta Woman's Club members, along with other clubwomen throughout the country, put forth an intense effort on behalf of soldiers. One of the most telling results of their efforts occurred when the Council of National Defense appointed GFWC president Ione V. H. Cowles and former GFWC president Eva Perry Moore to its newly created Woman's Committee. The General Federation established war service and editorial offices in Washington, DC, organized Red Cross units, and, in collaboration with the YMCA, created an overseas unit of about 100 young women to assist with the war effort. These activities reflected the clubwomen's growing influence in all aspects of United States' domestic and foreign policy, an influence never before imagined.[141]

The economic challenges of World War I forced many out of work. As a result of the efforts of the Atlanta Woman's Club, a Clearing House for the Unemployed grew out of an Emergency Association for Unemployed Women, directed by the Club's governing board. The agency's mission was to help competent women who had been thrown out of work by hard times. The Clearing House also aided men and boys connected to female applicants. Its endeavors were so successful the organiza-

138 1896–1920 scrapbook, *Atlanta Woman's Club Scrapbook Collection*, Finding Aid Mss 326–60, Kenan Research Center, Atlanta History Center.

139 Houde, *Reaching Out*, 157; 1896–1920 scrapbook, *Atlanta Woman's Club Scrapbook Collection*, Finding Aid MSS 326–60; "For Our Mutual Benefit"; "Atlanta Woman's Club 1," Atlanta Woman's Club Archives.

140 *Atlanta Woman's Club Scrapbook, 1896–1920*, Atlanta Woman's Club Scrapbook Collection, MSS 326–60, Kenan Research Center, Atlanta History Center, Atlanta GA.

141 "Timeline 2010," Women's History and Resource Center, General Federation of Women's Clubs, Washington, DC; Houde, "Reaching Out," 150–51.

142 1896–1920 scrapbook, *Atlanta Woman's Club Scrapbook Collection*, Finding Aid MSS 326–60, Kenan Research Center, Atlanta History Center; "How Women of Atlanta Helped to Pass the Last Big Bond Issue as Told by Mrs. Woods White," unidentified newspaper article, 1914, in 1896–1920 scrapbook.

143 1896–1920 scrapbook. *Atlanta Woman's Club Scrapbook Collection*, Kenan Research Center, Atlanta History Center.

144 Dinah Peevy, "Mary Ann Lipscomb," unpublished research paper, 2009, presented spring 2010 at Atlanta Woman's Club meeting.

145 "For Our Mutual Benefit"; Ada Beihl, "Woman's Club Celebrates 75th Year Serving City," *Atlanta Journal-Constitution*, 1 November 1970; Houde, *Reaching Out*, 132; "Against Women Lobbyists," unidentified newspaper article, 1 August 1912, in 1896–1920 scrapbook, *Atlanta Woman's Club Scrapbook Collection*, MSS 326–60, O'SZ3.74, 2nd scrapbook; "Woman's Clubs Offer Aid to Titanic Victims," unidentified newspaper article, 1911, in 1896–1920 scrapbook; Boutwell, Ann Taylor, "The Grand Old Lady," unidentified article copy, Wimbish House Archives, Atlanta Woman's Club 1.

tion added a Department of Vocational Guidance under the direction of Mr. George Halsy. The center created employment opportunities, sold the work of women who had to remain in their homes, and established a place of registry to bring potential employees and employers together. The Atlanta Woman's Club often collaborated with the Atlanta Chamber of Commerce in an effort to become one of the chamber's vital resources.[142]

In 1915, the Atlanta Woman's Club established a Committee on Peace and a new Committee on Markets, raised funds for Emory University through the City Federation, and continued to work to help the city's unemployed.[143]

In 1916, after two decades of tireless work by Atlanta Woman's Club members, other federation members, and child advocates, the Georgia General Assembly passed a weak compulsory education bill. The legislation required students between the ages of eight and fourteen to attend school twelve weeks a year.[144]

The Atlanta Woman's Club and other Federation clubs continued to present programs and work with other organizations to raise funds to improve medical facilities; endow new hospitals, sanitariums, and infirmaries; push for domestic science programs in schools; advocate vocational guidance and training; and promote the prevention and eradication of disease. Among the main beneficiaries was the American Red Cross. The women also supported legislation and appropriations for food and drug law enforcement. Among their other projects were spreading awareness of the value of historic preservation, endorsement of the Humane Society, and support of the passage of a resolution designed to prevent cruelty to animals. They also extended aid for victims of the Titanic through their membership in the Atlanta Federation; continued their support of the State Library Commission's rural traveling library program; endorsed the preservation of the Atlanta Civil War Cyclorama; and promoted native Georgia crafts.[145]

Atlanta Woman's Club members, along with those of the City and Georgia Federations, saw great success in their efforts but preferred to exert their influence through conservative means. Rather than overt lobbying, they limited their commu-

Mrs. Woods White
1911–1912

Mrs. A. P. Coles
1912–1914

Mrs. P. J. McGovern
1914–1916

Mrs. J. N. McEachern, Sr.
1916–1918

Mrs. Claude C. Smith
1918–1921

nication to influencing their husbands and their husbands' friends and to writing newspaper articles and letters.[146]

During 1917, the Executive Board of the GaFWC condemned lynching as a means of punishing crime of "any name or character."[147] In 1918, years of intense campaigning by Georgia clubwomen and other women's organizations culminated in University of Georgia Trustees approving the admission of women to junior-, senior-, and graduate-level courses.[148]

The Atlanta Woman's Club's demand for equal education for Georgia women focused members' attention on the Southern suffrage movement. Basing their theories on women's "physical weakness, inherent sensitivity and nervousness," anti-suffragists believed women were unfit for political life, but the more women achieved and the more confident they became, the more Atlanta Woman's Club members and other clubs sought greater independence and more political rights.[149]

Several activist women's organizations greatly influenced the Atlanta Woman's Club's efforts. One such organization was the Woman's Christian Temperance Union, which at the turn of the century was a major liberalizing force in the South. The women envied the power and influence enjoyed by the WCTU, the suffragists, and other groups, but following the General Federation's lead, AWC members stood back from radical feminist issues for fear of alienation. Instead, they focused their attention on local community building.[150]

In order to attract more Georgia women to their movement, suffragists pointed out the relationship between social reform and women's right to vote. Despite their efforts, the Atlanta Woman's Club and other Georgia clubwomen generally avoided any overt relationship with their suffragist counterparts.[151]

In 1919, during its state convention, the Georgia Federation endorsed equal suffrage. This was followed the next year by heightened discussion on the "Exercise of Franchise."[152] By this time, suffrage had already been passed by Congress. It is not surprising that the Atlanta Woman's Club was so conservative about overtly supporting women's issues. Members of the Georgia legislature detested the idea of granting rights to women.

Several energetic women led the Atlanta Woman's Club as it passed into and through the latter half of the century's second decade. Lending their expertise to the membership in this era were Mrs. Woods White (1911–1912), Mrs. A. P. Coles (1912–1914), Mrs. P. J. McGovern (1914–1916), Mrs. J. N. McEachern, Sr. (1916–1918), and Mrs. Claude C. Smith (1918–1921).[153]

146 "Against Women Lobbyists," unidentified newspaper article, 1 August 1912, Atlanta Woman's Club Scrapbook, 1896-1920. Kenan Research Center, Atlanta History Center.

147 Anderson, ed., "A Walk through History."

148 "For Our Mutual Benefit."

149 Ibid.

150 Roth, *Matronage: Patterns in Women's Organizations, Atlanta, Georgia, 1890–1940* (Brooklyn NY: Carlson Publishing Company, 1994) 8–10.

151 "For Our Mutual Benefit."

152 Anderson, ed., "A Walk through History."

153 "List of Presidents," paper, Atlanta Woman's Club Wimbish House Archives.

CHAPTER ELEVEN

No one not connected with this project will realize the hard work through the hot days, the rising at 4:30 in the morning to reach Produce Row in time to interview the farmers, the cross-country trips and the constant supervision necessary to see that the market was conducted in an honest and sanitary manner.

Atlanta Woman's Club member[154]

On Monday afternoon, 21 May 1917, a fire roared through the streets of Atlanta, destroying 300 acres of nearly 2,000 businesses, churches, and homes and killing a woman who suffered a heart attack. Lasting until almost midnight, the conflagration raged for over a mile along Edgewood Avenue, into Sweet Auburn, and across Ponce de Leon, leaving more than 10,000 people displaced and losses totaling over $5 million.[155]

Atlanta has a history of rising from the ashes, and the aftermath of the fire of 1917 was no exception. Little remained of the dwellings on Edgewood Avenue, but it was on that scarred and blackened land Atlanta's first enclosed Municipal Market would be built.[156]

The Atlanta Woman's Club members had never forgotten their goal of establishing a permanent farmer's market. An *Atlanta Journal* article dated 11 November 1917 refers to Atlanta Woman's Club member Nellie Peters Black, stating, "With the war beginning in 1914 and with Georgia's relation as a cotton producing state to Germany's commerce, there was an

---

154 Atlanta Woman's Club Biennial Report—1966–1968, p. 47, folder box, MSS 353, Kenan Research Center, Atlanta History Center, Atlanta GA.

155 "Great Atlanta Fire of 1917," Digital Library of Georgia, contributor, Atlanta History Center, Kenan Research Center, 2006.

156 "Atlanta's Sweet Auburn Curb Market Carries On," *Edible Metro & Mountains*, www.ediblecommunities.com/metroandmountains/fall-2009/historic-urban (accessed 29 December 2009).

impetus given the agricultural campaign work. Mrs. Nellie Peters Black, then a member of the Agricultural Committee of the Georgia Federation of Women's Clubs, organized a series of agricultural rallies which she assembled with the aid of club women of the twelve districts." The article further states that Mrs. Black invited to the rallies agricultural experts from the College of Agriculture and other cooperating government and state agencies. During one trip through the state, Mrs. Black addressed a total of 28,000 attendants at 28 meetings.

The Club president and chairman of the Market Committee visited a number of cities to study public marketing in other areas. They also secured the help of the State Bureau of Markets and the State Agricultural College. Several months before the opening, club committees toured the surrounding countryside to notify farmers that the curb market would be opening. They urged them to plant vegetables and fruits that could be profitable. Posters were placed along all roads leading out of Atlanta, and in 1918 an open-air market was established on a fire-razed plot.

Atlanta Woman's Club members, dressed in farmerette (a term generally known as referring to women who helped their husbands on farms) attire, worked the curbside vegetable stand at the corner of the Peachtrees from 4:30 AM until dusk. Factory workers were among their best customers. For several weeks after the curb market was started, committees for the Woman's Club, assisted by the American Legion and Junior League, stationed themselves on the city's outskirts to direct farmers to the market. Under the Market Committee's direction, lectures were given related to introducing new food crops. As the boll weevil ravaged Southern cotton, Georgia's agriculture was marked by a shift to fruit and vegetable crops resulting in highly improved farming conditions and a bigger emphasis on the purchase of Georgia homegrown products.

The endeavor realized a tremendous return in dollars and cents as it impacted the entire city and surrounding territory. The market's success was known not only in Georgia, but also in other states where similar projects were soon begun. Sales grew from a few hundred dollars a day to thousands, with annual sales of many hundreds of thousands of dollars. Consumers realized tremendous savings by purchasing homegrown produce rather than having to pay higher prices which included the expense of importing products from other states, including freight rates. Unsold products were donated to charities.

The thriving enterprise was soon enclosed by a tent. The Atlanta curb market was so successful it was outgrowing its humble beginnings. Farmers had increased production and diversified crops, but revenue often depended on the weather. Millions of dollars in food crops were still shipped into Georgia, and freight costs and overhead siphoned off monies that might otherwise have remained in the state. At a time when the cost of living was rising, something had to be done.

The Atlanta Woman's Club and other city organizations noted the market's success and pushed for a fireproof permanent home. After waging a "long war" through constant attendance at city council meetings, Atlanta Woman's Club members raised capital for seed money; the City of Atlanta allocated $85,000 to purchase the property; and A. Ten Eyck Brown, a prominent early twentieth-century architect, was commissioned to design the structure. Their efforts resulted in a brick and concrete building covering an entire city block. Located in the city's exact geographical center, the Municipal Market of Atlanta opened in May 1924 and soon became the state's largest farmer's market. At the time, the project was deemed one of the most important ever launched by the Atlanta Woman's Club.

The facility brought in thousands of dollars in produce sales. Items sold included "vegetables, fruits, chickens, butter, eggs, buttermilk, meal, cider, syrup, honey, ham, and herbs." Winter months saw sales of "sausage, spareribs, rabbits, squirrels" and "game, sugar cane, and nuts." Other enterprises included sales of "jellies, jams, canned products and flowers." The market was soon serving over tens of thousands of customers monthly with unsold perishables often continuing to be donated to local charities.[157]

When the Atlanta Woman's Club began the push for a market, they had no idea their project would become a permanent Atlanta institution. According to researcher Darlene Rebecca Roth, for a while club members continued to accept some responsibilities for the market's success, such as operating a rummage stall inside the market, keeping watch over the building, and petitioning local government for improvements. Gradually they relinquished control until the market fared well on its own.[158]

Although urban renewal programs, the popularity of the suburbs, and massive supermarkets took their toll, the market, renovated in 1994 as the Sweet Auburn Curb Market, retains its early appeal. Approaching ninety years in operation, the facility is still a prosperous business.

The Atlanta Woman's Club had entered the twentieth century with a membership yearning for social reform, but, according to Darlene Roth, club members continued to embrace a passionate acceptance of what it meant to be a Southern woman. The membership emphasized purpose and duty—duty to home, family, community, state, county, race, and God. For most, this meant a more passive role than their confrontational suffragist counterparts. As the suffrage movement gained strength and women's right to vote came closer to reality, they invited suffragists to present programs. But it was not until 1919, after the Susan B. Anthony Amendment was passed, that AWC women were spurred to action. Upon Anthony's endorsement, Georgia's women's clubs prepared their members for voting, wrote articles for local newspapers, conducted citizenship classes, and sponsored lectures on parliamentary law.

For members of the Atlanta Woman's Club, the pursuit of equal political rights was frightening, not only because of the knowledge and responsibilities such freedoms demanded, but also because of the threat they posed to women's traditional roles. Most women felt safer in their paternalistic male-dominated society, as many still do today, aligning with their husbands' and fathers' political ideas and prejudices even when those prejudices work against them. However, as the years progressed, the push for equal education became the "springboard" for Georgia women to support equal voting rights. The relationship between politics and the ability to promote social reform added the final push, but only after women thought the granting of the right to vote was assured. Sadly, Georgia was the first state to veto the Susan B. Anthony Bill. The state did not formally ratify the amendment until 1970.[159]

[157] "Mrs. Nellie Peters Black," Article, Wimbish House Archives; Atlanta Woman's Club Archive Notes, Wimbish House Archives; Sapero, Cynthia (first vice president, Atlanta Woman's Club, 1998–2000), "The Atlanta Woman's Club . . . Our History," Wimbish House Archives; "Atlanta's Sweet Auburn Market," Atlanta Woman's Club Souvenir Book, 1922–1923, pp. 13–14, MSS 326–60, Kenan Research Center, Atlanta History Center, Atlanta GA; "Woman's Club to Start Drive for Permanent Market Building Here," unidentified article, 1920, MSS 353, Scrapbook #18, ovz 3.39, Kenan Research Center; "Atlanta's Curb Market; Its Value and Effect," unidentified article, MSS 353, Scrapbook #18 ovz 3.39; "Atlanta's Sweet Auburn Curb Market"; Project for Public Spaces, "Sweet Auburn Club Market," Great Public Spaces, www.pps.org/great_public_spaces/one?public_place_id=182 (29 December 2009); Atlanta Woman's Club Biennial Report, 1966–1968, pp.47–48, MSS 535; Boutwell, Ann Taylor, "The Grand Old Lady," unidentified newspaper article, Wimbish House Archives; Atlanta Woman's Club Souvenir Book 1922–1923, p 13, MSS 353; unidentified article, Scrapbook #18 ,ovz 3.39, MSS 353, Atlanta History Center; "Market Campaign Will Be Launched by Woman's Club," 14 Jun 1924, unidentified article, MSS 353, Scrapbook #18, ovz 3.39, Kenan Research Center.

[158] Roth, *Matronage: Patterns In Women's Organizations, Atlanta, Georgia, 1890–1940* (Brooklyn: Carlson Publishing, 1994) 59–60.

159 "For Our Mutual Benefit: The Athens Woman's Club and Social Reform, 1899–1920," no date, Athens Woman's Club collection, Heritage Room, Athens-Clarke County Library, Athens GA, Digital Library of Georgia/GALILEO (Athens GA: University of Georgia Libraries, 2006–2007), dlg.galileo.usg.edu/athenswomansclub (accessed 12 October 2009).

160 Franklin M. Garrett, *Atlanta and its Environs*, vol. 2 (New York: Lewis Historical Pub. Co., 1954, 1987) 761–62, in collection at Kenan Research Center.

161 Ibid., 764.

Spurred by a sense of growing power, members of the Atlanta Woman's Club took on projects that had tremendous impact on Atlanta's growth. Concerned about their city's quality of life, they seized opportunities to enhance and promote its citizens' well-being. Society was rapidly changing, and the clubwomen found themselves torn between embracing new technological developments and working to offset the sometimes negative consequences these advancements brought about. Among the women's ongoing concerns was the moral effect of mainstream movies on children. Both the General Federation and the Atlanta Woman's Club monitored these films and their influence.

The women also remained concerned about the war and the soldiers who served. In 1918, Atlanta's more elite young women, known as "useful war debutantes," could be found at tea dances held at the Club: "Dances for officers were going strong at the AWC on Baker Street, and each young lady attending had to present her admission card at the door. High fashion for femininity called for skirts touching high-topped laced or button shoes for daytime, and extremely pointed pumps ornamented with big buckles for afternoon wear. Close-fitting turbans, peg-top dresses, wide-brimmed velvet and duvetyn hats embroidered in gold and silver threads, pocketbooks suspended from bracelets and satin dresses were all the rage." When a reception was held for the wife of World War I hero Sgt. Alvin York, Mrs. York "wore a blue dress and black velvet picture hat."[160]

As the war scaled down, the Atlanta Woman's Club focused again on hopes for peace. Members endorsed President Woodrow Wilson's plans for a League of Nations and sponsored programs on international affairs.[161]

Atlanta Woman's Club members attending their Spring Tea 2010

Atlanta Woman's Club leaders attending the Spring Tea 2010: Front (seated) left to right: Karen Clydesdale, Lucy Willard, Sarah Helen Killgore, Daisy Luckey Aukermann; back from left to right: Myra Carmon, Lisa Banes, Karen Bacheller, Karen Thomson, Barbara Culmer-Ilaw, Sandra McNeil

Atlanta Woman's Club Spring Tea 2010, (left to right) Karen Bacheller, John Bacheller, Dr. Candace Kaspers, 2009 Atlanta Woman's Club Retreat Leader on Team Building

Attendees at the Atlanta Woman's Club Spring Tea 2010 in Wimbish House Ballroom

Attendees at the Atlanta Woman's Club Spring Tea 2010 (from left to right): Lucy Willard, Rose Ditto, Sandra McNeil, Gewene Womack, Chair, Board of Trustees, Tallullah Falls School

Presidents attending the Atlanta Woman's Club Spring Tea 2010 (from front to back): Dr. Rose Ditto, International GFWC President 2008-2010; Brenda Martin, GaFWC President 2008-2010; Dr. Karen Thomson, Atlanta Woman's Club President 2008-2010; Karen Bacheller, Atlanta Woman's Club President 2010-2012

Gift to Rose Ditto on Behalf of Atlanta Woman's Club by Atlanta Woman's Club President Karen Thomson

Myra Carmon

Karen Clydesdale

Barbara Culmer-Ilaw

Betty Daniels

Emily Grigsby

Judine Heard

Sarah Helen Killgore

Sandra McNeil

Barbara Roberts

Louise Vernon

Lucy Willard

Ruth Yurchuck

Daisy Luckey Aukerman at the Steinway piano upstairs prior to the Atlanta Woman's Club General Meeting, May 2010

Collecting money for lunch prior to Atlanta Woman's Club business (General) meeting, May 2010

Guest artists perform African drumming and dancing with member Marilyn Morton at Atlanta Woman's Club General Meeting, May 2010

Margaret Frost and Page Henry at Atlanta Woman's Club General Meeting, May 2010

CHAPTER TWELVE

A criminal may reform, but once a female, always a female.

Mrs. Ida Clyde Clarke[162]

he Atlanta Woman's Club's membership soon outgrew its Baker Street clubhouse and sought more expansive headquarters. In 1919, due to members' ingenuity, vision and commitment, the Club was able to purchase a Peachtree Street mansion to be their home. Under the direction of Club president Mrs. Claude C. Smith (1918–1921), members sold their old clubhouse for $35,000 and purchased the large and architecturally unique residence from William A. Wimbish for $47,500.

Years before, Mr. Wimbish and his wife visited with friends in turn-of-the-century Southern France and they became enamored with their friends' beautiful sandstone French Chateau. They were so impressed, Mr. Wimbish decided to build a home patterned in its likeness.[163]

In September 1903, Mr. Wimbish purchased four city lots just south of 14th Street adjoining Peachtree Street and Crescent Avenue. Eliminating the alleyway between the lots, he formed a single parcel fronting Peachtree. In early 1906, he purchased a building permit for the house and hired one of the South's most prominent architects, Walter Thomas Downing, to draw the plans.[164]

---

162 Mrs. Ida Clyde Clarke, quoting Britain's Lady Rhondda on why she was barred from the English House of Lords, unknown article source, in Muriel Mellawn, "Lady Rhondda and the Changing Faces of British Feminism," *Frontiers: A Journal of Women Studies* 9/2 (1987): 7–13.

163 Atlanta Woman's Club History #1, paper, Wimbish House Archives, Atlanta GA; Willifard, William Bailey, "Peachtree's Residential Twilight," from *Peachtree Street, Atlanta*, Wimbish House Archives; Bryant, Mrs. Curtis H., "History of the Atlanta Woman's Club," notes, Atlanta Woman's Club Archives, Wimbish House; "The Atlanta Woman's Club Celebrates 100 Years," *Northside Neighbor*, 8 Nov 1995, B2, Wimbish House Archives.

164 Typed papers, source unknown, Wimbish House Archives.

165 Biennial Report, Atlanta Woman's Club, 1944–1946, p. 63, folder box, MSS 326–60, Kenan Research Center, Atlanta History Center, Atlanta GA.

166 "The Atlanta Woman's Club," www.atlwc.org (accessed October 2009); Atlanta Woman's Club Bulletin 1922, Wimbish House Archives; 1895 scrapbook, *Atlanta Woman's Club Scrapbook Collection*, MSS 326–60, Kenan Research Center; "History of the Atlanta Woman's Club: Its Growth and Resultful Achievements," Atlanta Woman's Club Souvenir Book, pp. 3–7, Wimbish House Archives; Elizabeth Mac Lyon, *Victorian Heritage* (Atlanta: Atlanta Historical Society, 1976), in archives at Kenan Research Center; McAlister, *A Field Guide to American Houses* (New York: Alfred A. Knopf, 1985), Kenan Research Center; Southern Historical Association, *Memoirs of Georgia, Historical and Biographical*, 2 vols., Atlanta, 1895, Kenan Research Center.

167 Bryant, "History of the Atlanta Woman's Club," Wimbish House Archives.

In his rendition of the Wimbish House, Downing presented a chateauesque design that makes the home unique in the context of Atlanta's architectural heritage. The hipped roof was steeply pitched and truncated by a flat roof deck with ornamental metal cresting and finials. It included a turret and short tower with candle-snuffer roof and steep parapeted gables over wall dormers that extended all the way through the cornice line and thick limestone walls in the main body of the house. The original structure, completed in 1906, boasted just over 6,000 square feet on the two main floors. The lot contained 123 feet of frontage on Peachtree Street, running back 340 feet. The beautiful home and its grounds originally cost $75,000, but the clubwomen were able to purchase it for $42,500. The structure was built of white sandstone, with a white castle-like trim of wood, and was surrounded by green grass, large water oaks, and flowering shrubs. The house was built for comfort and grace, with high-ceilinged rooms, mahogany-trimmed woodwork, and six upstairs bedrooms.[165]

To meet the Club's new expenses, annual dues were increased from $5 to $10 and the initiation fee from $2 to $5. The additional dues, along with other revenue, enabled club members to pay $12,500 on the new clubhouse in the first year. Thirty women were invited to become life members at $100 each, which supplied $3,000 toward furnishings and other necessary equipment.[166]

According to former Atlanta Woman's Club president Mrs. Curtis H. Bryant (1982–1984), the original Wimbish home had a covered porch on the front with an open porch leading to the right side of the house and a covered portico with a high step for people disembarking carriages. The front door opened into an entrance hall, flanked by beautiful circular columns; a huge circular parlor, with gaslights, an open fireplace and tall curved glass windows; a glass-enclosed sunroom the women called the "Palm Room"; a spacious library; a huge dining room with adjoining butler's pantry; and a stairway to the kitchen area.

The center of the entrance hall was adorned with a magnificent curved, hand-carved stairway that led to a decorative second-floor landing equipped with lights for portraits and paintings. Four large bedrooms and baths opened onto the landing. Another bedroom, living room, and bath opened from the stairway and afforded a separate living area for servants. All of the rooms were circular. The stairs leading down from the center of the main building led to a wide hallway and on to what may have been a formal garden adjoining the downstairs quarters, which included additional rooms, perhaps used by the kitchen staff.

Every room contained a fireplace with a small hatch for dropping coal ashes downstairs, and there was a huge coal bin off the driveway. The furnace room, located down a cement stairwell, contained three huge fireplaces. Later, there was a boiler, probably installed by the Woman's Club, which created steam for iron steam heaters in the main rooms. Other more modern heating systems were installed as the years went by.[167]

Shortly after moving into the Wimbish House, the Club's membership soared over 1,000. The clubhouse was adequate for committee meetings, executive offices, and departmental activities, but there was no place for such a large membership to convene. The club soon began a campaign to raise funds to build an auditorium. A chairman and forty captains were appointed along with a building committee, and at

The Wimbish House today   *Photograph: Artstar by Laura Stone*

168 Sapero, "The Atlanta Woman's Club . . . Our History"; "History of the Atlanta Woman's Club: Its Growth and Resultful Achievements," 3–7. Wimbish House Archives.

169 "Notes," Atlanta Woman's Club Wimbish House Archives. Atlanta Woman's Club Bulletin, 1922, Wimbish House Archives; Atlanta Woman's Club Scrapbooks, MSS 326–60, Kenan Research Center; Bryant, "History of the Atlanta Woman's Club," typed notes, Atlanta Woman's Club Archives; "History of the Atlanta Woman's Club: Its Growth and Resultful Achievements," 3–7.

170 "History of the Atlanta Woman's Club: Its Growth and Resultful Achievements," 3–7.

the end of two months, $18,000 in cash and pledges were raised. A citizen, Mr. Manget, started the contributions with a gift of $2,000, and three others contributed $1,000 each. Two gifts of $500 and one of $250 were made, and retailers each gave $100. The rest was raised by the membership. Atlanta's newspapers supported the drive through unlimited publicity and urged the public, as responsible citizens, to make contributions.[168]

As the campaign continued, club members were asked to contribute $45 each, and the Club hired architects P. Thornton Marye and Barrett Alger. The Club members held numerous fundraisers, including card parties, dances, moving-picture programs, sales of various items including aprons and millinery products, journalism classes, lectures, pageants, plays, opera musicales, teas, banquets, a cooking school, a Tom Thumb wedding, and other initiatives. The two architects prepared a master plan that included renovations and the addition of an auditorium, a banquet hall, and a rectangular swimming pool.[169]

Despite the clubwomen's projects, they still needed $60,000 to complete the plans. Unfortunately, this was a time when the nation's business boom waned, creating financial panic. Despite the difficulties even large, established businesses experienced in creating cash flow, the women refused to relent. Finally, the Volunteer State Life Insurance Company agreed to offer the loan. The transaction was a gender milestone as it was the largest loan ever acquired by a woman's organization in the South.[170]

The property of the Atlanta Woman's Club, without the auditorium, was appraised at between $70,000 and $80,000. The auditorium would add $110,000 to make nearly $200,000 worth of property backing a loan of $60,000. To fund the loan,

171 Atlanta Woman's Club History #1, Wimbish House Archives; Boutwell, Ann Taylor, "The Grand Old Lady," unidentified article copy, Wimbish House Archives; "Papers," Atlanta Woman's Club Wimbish House Archives. Atlanta Woman's Club Bulletin, 1922, Wimbish House Archives; Atlanta Woman's Club Scrapbooks, MSS 326–60, Kenan Research Center; Lyon, *Victorian Heritage*; McAlester, *Field Guide to American Houses*; Southern Historical Association, *Memoirs of Georgia*; Bryant, "History of the Atlanta Woman's Club"; "History of the Atlanta Woman's Club: Its Growth and Resultful Achievements," 3–7; Atlanta Woman's Club History #1; unidentified news clipping, p. 81, Women's Club Scrapbook, beginning 1921, Wimbish House Archives.

172 "Curtain to Be Drawn on *Democracy de Luxe* in Gem-Like Theater," unidentified news clipping, p.79, Women's Club Scrapbook, beginning 1921, Wimbish House Archives.

173 Atlanta Woman's Club Bulletin, 1922; Atlanta Woman's Club Scrapbooks, MSS 326–60, Kenan Research Center.

the Club took $60,000 in fifteen-year endowment insurance on forty-seven of its members. The policies were to have a cash value at the end of the fifteen years totaling $60,000. The women obtained their money and the insurance company made a secure loan and, in the process, gained publicity.

At the time they purchased the Wimbish House, the Atlanta Woman's Club membership included women of such power and influence that they were able to raise nearly $175,000 over the next five years for major construction projects. Mr. W. P. Frances was hired as the building's contractor, and in May 1921, the Club held a Masonic cornerstone ceremony for the Lucille King Thomas Auditorium, dedicating the building to their Club's president for her untiring work. Dues were increased to $15 with an initiation fee of $10, and fifteen additional life members were added at $150 each. The project was completed in 1922. The auditorium was elegant in design, lavishly decorated, and included spacious aisles and seating arrangements in the orchestra and balconies. Its entrance opened into a marble foyer where steps on each side led to the balcony. Slanting floors focused attention on the stage, which, large enough to accommodate 200 seats, held footlights, a proscenium drop curtain, and other necessary equipment. The space beneath the stage housed lockers and dressing rooms. In front of the stage an orchestra pit was bordered by boxes, each with seating for eight. Seven hundred overstuffed, comfortable chairs were installed in the main auditorium and balcony, with room for three hundred more in the aisles and foyer. The entire building was equipped with sprinklers and up-to-date fans for cooling and warming. Special attention was paid to the building's acoustics, with the idea of projecting women's voices. This was a very progressive move, considering that when the Club was formed, few women were even allowed to speak in public.[171]

The auditorium's opening play was *Democracy de Luxe*. Its author, the renowned dramatist Parker Hord, gave the following synopsis: "It is a present-day story of life among the social and diplomatic set of the national capital, and although the setting is American and Louis Morrison plays the part of a young newspaper reporter with all the exuberance of a Douglas Fairbanks, there is even more of the old-world element than is supplied by the titled emissaries from foreign countries.

"Two royal refugees continue here their love story begun in one of those little kingdoms not to be located on the maps of our geographies, but well enough designated by saying it is 'somewhere east of the setting sun.'" Leading roles were played by two talented Atlanta actresses, Miss Erskine Jarnagin and Mrs. Ulric Atkinson. Following the play, there was an after-theater supper.[172]

The event attracted many prominent Georgians, including Governor and Mrs. Thomas Hardwick and Mayor and Mrs. James L. Key. The auditorium's opening was said to represent "a monumental achievement" surpassing the "cost of erection and beauty of every other women's club auditorium in the United States . . . [and] stands foremost as a conspicuous achievement of the club women." The theatre became well known for its excellent acoustics and intimate scale as "one of the most unique buildings in America in that it was built to serve a dual purpose—an auditorium where sunlight may penetrate and to be used when meetings, lectures, and the like are held, and a modern theatre when this is desired."[173]

Built mainly to accommodate the Atlanta clubwomen, the auditorium also fulfilled Atlanta's need for an appropriate venue to hold concerts, lectures, plays, and other cultural events. Upon its opening, the facility quickly became the center of the city's artistic life, serving as the springboard for the formation of many of Atlanta's cultural and fine arts programs. It signaled the beginning of the city's legitimate theater and provided steady revenue for the Club through rental fees for conventions, concerts, lectures, plays, recitals, and films. The Atlanta Woman's Club also frequently hosted local artists in concert performances, thereby sponsoring the city's musical community. Over the years, the auditorium's service as a multifaceted facility included its role as a temporary home to the Peachtree Playhouse and, in recent years, to the Petrus, Axyz, and Eleven 50 nightclubs.[174]

In September 1922, club members began another campaign to build a large banquet hall to connect the house and the auditorium; they immediately raised $18,000. Following their loan-making precedent, the Volunteer State Life Insurance Company insured eighteen additional members for a loan of $18,000, and, on 23 April 1923, that new facility was dedicated. The property was soon teeming with activity as members and visitors enjoyed the facilities, which eventually included tennis courts and an art gallery on the main floor.[175]

In recent years, AWC member and president Cynthia Sapero (2000–2002) understood the reasoning and purposes behind the needs and determination of the club members. In an excerpt from her writings, she states, "The Wimbish House complex represents a time when women's organizations sought 'homes' for their activities rather than offices. It is no coincidence that the organization ran its affairs from a house, outfitted the house with a large kitchen and meeting space, nor that the whole of the complex was located in a residential rather than commercial area. The intention was to have the home of the organization speak as an extension of woman's role—from the home of the individual to the home out in the community."[176]

According to Mrs. Sapero, the complete complex represents a period of strong commitment on the part of the women to community service, with much effort and capital put into the structures. The theater was large enough to hold statewide meetings, host summer stock productions, and serve as home to the "Theater of the Stars" for decades. The swimming pool satisfied a neighborhood need until it was eventually closed and filled in. Particularly since the 1960s, the membership of the Woman's Club has dwindled considerably, but the organization continues to work for community charities, with emphasis on those for women and children. The massive changes that swept through Midtown since World War I left sites such as the Wimbish House ripe for targets of land speculators, and most succumbed to the pressures. Due to financial need and in an effort to preserve its historic premises, the Atlanta Woman's Club leased out the theater in 1989 to Petrus, which ran a nightclub there for several years. What was once the theater used for recitals, concerts, and other cultural events in the twentieth century was renovated in the first decade of the twenty-first century as a European opera house and currently operates as a nightclub called "Opera." It was voted the best Dance Club in Atlanta in summer 2008. Further, Opera has been used as the set for the television series "The Real

[174] "History of the Atlanta Woman's Club: Its Growth and Resultful Achievements," 3–7; Atlanta Woman's Club Souvenir Book, 1922–1923, pp. 7–10, MSS 326–60; Ada Biehl, "Woman's Club Celebrates 75th Year Serving City, *Atlanta Journal-Constitution*, 1 Nov 1970, Wimbish House Archives; Ann Taylor Boutwell, "The Grand Old Lady"; Roth and Shaw, "From Center Stage to Center Court," *Atlanta Women: From Myth to Modern Times, A Century of History*, (Atlanta: Atlanta History Society, 1980), HQ 1439. A7 R67, Atlanta History Center, Atlanta GA.

[175] "Manget Gives $2,000 to Fund for Woman's Club Auditorium," unidentified article, Scrapbook #18, p. 3, 1955–56, "Highlights & Outstanding Events of AWC Life Members," MSS 353, Kenan Research Center.

[176] Sapero, "Atlanta Woman's Club," papers, Wimbish House Archives.

Housewives of Atlanta" and continues to accommodate other such special purposes and events.

For more than sixty years, beginning in 1924, the theater of the Atlanta Woman's Club was renowned for its concerts, recitals, plays, and other cultural programs. Mrs. Sapero has stated, "With its prestigious Peachtree Street address and spacious and accommodating facilities, the home of the Atlanta Woman's Club became the site of meetings and events of other women's clubs and a gathering place for civic events, and the arts. AWC members graciously lent leadership, expertise and hospitality for conventions and other important occasions."[177]

177 Sapero, "Atlanta Woman's Club," papers, Wimbish House Archives.

*The untiring efforts of the women of the Atlanta Woman's Club
have, against tremendous odds, helped to preserve for posterity one
of the city's most unique architectural and historical landmarks.*

Cynthia Sapero[178]

uring the early 1920s, the Atlanta Woman's Club endured the
challenges of expansion and fundraising while continuing to
focus on educating members, promoting the welfare of the
community, and lending support and resources to those in
isolated areas. In her President's Address, Mrs. Irving Thomas (1920–1921)
refers to the Atlanta Woman's Club as the "great loving mother" of the
Atlanta community, standing for "truth, justice, mercy and love." As for the
members, "You touch and heal." With the passage of the Susan B. Anthony
bill and reflecting their new roles as intelligent voters, the Club took an
enthusiastic interest in citizenship.[179] The Club also established an exten-
sive library within the Wimbish House. Of the thousands of carefully
selected volumes, the favorites were works by Jane Austen and Charles
Dickens.

The women continued to cooperate with the General and State
Federations, collaborating on national and state issues including the condition and treatment of Native Americans. The General Federation of
Women's Clubs was a longtime advocate of Native American rights and
had long promoted improvements in education and healthcare on reservations and preservation of Native American culture. In 1921, the GFWC
created an Indian Welfare Committee.

178 "Atlanta Woman's Club," Wimbish House Archives, Atlanta GA.

179 Irving, Mrs. Thomas S., *26th Yearbook of The Atlanta Woman's Club, Atlanta, Georgia*, 1920–1921, pp.
5–9, Wimbish House Archives.

180 "Timeline 2010," Women's History and Resource Center, General Federation of Women's Clubs, Washington, DC; 1921–1923 scrapbook, Wimbish House Archives.

181 "Resolutions," unidentified news clipping, p.82, Women's Club Scrapbook, beginning 1921, Wimbish House Archives.

182 1921–1923 scrapbook. Women's Club Scrapbooks, Wimbish House Archives

183 "The Atlanta Woman's Club Celebrates 100 Years," *Northside Neighbor*, 8 Nov 1995, B2, Wimbish House Archives.

184 Unidentified news clipping, p. 100, Women's Club Scrapbook, beginning 1921; Atlanta Woman's Club Souvenir Yearbook 1922–1923, p 16, MSS 326–60, Kenan Research Center, Atlanta History Center, Atlanta GA.

185 Ibid., 15–17; Atlanta Woman's Club Souvenir Book, p. 10, MSS 326–60.

The Atlanta Woman's Club followed the Federation's lead by endorsing citizenship legislation on behalf of the American Indian in letters to William D. Upshaw and Thomas Watson, Georgia members of the United States House of Representatives and Senate. Both responded with a pledge to action.[180]

The Club also took a stand on local issues of religious discrimination. Members adopted a resolution denouncing as un-American and detrimental to the best interests of Atlanta another group's attempt to bar Catholic teachers from local public schools.[181]

In October 1921, at the request of the Woman's Board of the Atlanta Chamber of Commerce, Atlanta Woman's Club members entertained President and Mrs. Warren Harding at a reception in their honor. On November 14, the Club was visited by Mrs. W.G. Winter, president of the General Federation. The Club continued to support organizations such as the Humane Society, the Red Cross, and the American Legion; sponsor children's Saturday morning matinees; work in hospitals and jails; and aid child welfare programs.[182]

One of the Club's projects was the continuation of their co-op exchange program allowing women living in remote areas to sell their crafts and earn income while working from home.[183] Products such as tufted bedspreads, pillow slips, runners, card table sets, luncheon sets, baby clothes, aprons, handkerchiefs, woven rugs, handmade laces, and hand-painted novelties were among the offerings.

Aware that many were at a loss as to how to choose and make popular items, the clubwomen sent recommendations and instructions to rural women through the mail so the women's work could bring them the highest profit. By June the next year, the Club had received 500 letters and collected $400 for the handiwork of women in rural districts. Over the years, the Club added other participants to the Exchange, including veterans.[184]

Because of the Atlanta Woman's Club's unrelenting commitment to improving life in the home, it became known as a "University for Homemakers." The Home Economics Department held monthly meetings; presented programs with national, state, and local speakers; arranged trips to local manufacturers; participated in exhibitions; fostered buy-at-home movements; and demonstrated labor-saving devices. Laboratory work was performed in home economics classes, and courses were offered in such subjects as interior decorating, sewing, millinery, cooking, and home management. In cooperation with downtown merchants, the department established a downtown "Playroom" managed by members and with the purpose of taking care of children while their mothers shopped. The endeavor was supported by fees from mothers and merchants.[185] In 1921, the Department compiled and published the *Atlanta Woman's Club Cookbook*, which within a year brought in $6,500 and was distributed all over the world. Today it can be found on the internet and the cookbook itself can be purchased online. Among the book's illustrious contributors were Mrs. Warren G. Harding and Mrs. Joel Chandler Harris.

EXCERPTS FROM THE
ATLANTA WOMAN'S CLUB 1921 COOKBOOK

RECIPES FROM FAMOUS HOMES *from Chapter IV*

The Home Economics Department of the Atlanta Woman's Club wishes to express its deep appreciation for the recipes contributed by "The First Lady of the Land," Mrs. Warren G. Harding, [an honorary member of the Atlanta Woman's Club], by the wives of so many of our governors, and by other notables.

MRS. HARDING'S CHICKEN PIE

1 Good-sized chicken	1 Qt. Flour
6 Small potatoes	1 Qt. Flour
1 Onion	1 T-spoon Salt
5 Level T-spoon Baking Powder	Milk

Boil chicken gently until it falls from bones; cut in small pieces. Cook potatoes and onion in chicken broth. Make a pastry of flour, lard, salt and baking powder—add milk enough to make a soft dough. Line baking dish with pastry and bake in hot oven. Then fill this with the chicken, potatoes, and a small amount of broth, cover with pastry and brown in quick oven. Thicken remaining broth, and serve over pie.

FROZEN FRUIT CAKE

1 Cup White raisins	1 Cup Macaroons
1 Cup Chopped pecans	1 Pt. Whipped cream
1 Cup Lady fingers	1 Pt. Boiled custard

Break lady fingers and macaroons in large crumbs. Put raisins in whole. Cut nuts in quarters. Whip the cream slightly. Mix all together lightly with pint of boiled custard. To freeze: put mixture in mold (with hole in center). Cover contents with waxed paper. Put lid on mold. Pack well. Let it remain packed three-and-one-half hours. When ready to serve, pour hot water over mold. Slide on platter. Pour glass of eggnog in hole in center.

—Mrs. Joel Chandler Harris, "Wren's Nest," Atlanta, Georgia

STEAMED HUCKLEBERRY PUDDING (from GEORGIA)

1 Qt. Berries	1½ Cups Milk
1 Cup Syrup (Georgia cane)	¾ T-spoon Soda
½ T-spoon Salt	Flour

Wash and dry berries; flour them as if for fruit cake. Stir soda into syrup; add milk and salt; add flour sufficient to make very stiff batter. Carefully stir in berries—avoid breaking them; put in greased steamer or mold; steam three hours, and serve with hard sauce.

—Mrs. Hugh Dorsey, Wife of former Governor of Georgia

BREAKFASTS *from Chapter VIII*
FRUITS IN SEASON
MRS. NORMAN SHARP—CHAIRMAN CITY MARKET
Most essential from the standpoint of hygiene is the inclusion of fruit in the daily diet, and this in Atlanta is a simple matter, for farmers supplying Atlanta's Municipal Curb Market furnish a continuous rotation of fruits during this entire year.

BAKED SHREDDED WHEAT
Shredded wheat is delicious, when divided into two parts by a sharp knife, each part being buttered, placed in the oven and heated till crisp. It tastes very much like popcorn, and may be eaten as a sandwich or with milk and sugar.

−Mrs. Newton C. Wing

ONE OF MRS. THORNTON'S FAVORITE BREAKFAST DISHES

1 Cup Meal	1½ Cups Well-cooked grits or hominy
½ Cup Boiling water	1 Cup Milk
1 Tbls Royal baking powder	3 Eggs
Butter size of walnut	Salt to taste

Put in mixing bowl butter, salt, meal, hominy and milk; mash fine, beat a few minutes, then stir in hot water. Add eggs, baking powder and beat well. Bake in shallow pan.

−Mrs. Albert Thornton, President, Atlanta City Federation of Women's Clubs

MRS. THOMAS' FAVORITE RECIPES *from Chapter XI*
Mrs. Irving Thomas, President of the Atlanta Woman's Club for three years, and elected Honorary Life President at the expiration of her term of office, is famed as well for her cookery as for her leadership in civic affairs. In answer to many requests for her recipes, she has given her favorites herewith. It is fitting that these should occupy a special chapter, both because they are all so delicious, and because the Auditorium, for which the proceeds from this book's sale will be used, is known as the Lucile King Thomas Auditorium.

SUGARED PECANS

1 Cup Pecans (meats)	1 Cup Granulated sugar
½ Cup Water	1 Cup Sugar XXXX

Boil granulated sugar and water to soft ball degree, drop pecans (one at a time) in hot syrup, dip out, roll separately in powdered sugar which has been sprinkled generously on a marble slab—lay on waxed paper.

CHICKEN SALAD

2½ Cups White meat chicken   1½ Cups Mayonnaise
1½ Cups Celery   1½ Cups Almonds (shelled)
1½ Cups Malaga grapes

Use white meat of chicken from above recipe, peel and remove seed from grapes, cut celery in small pieces, cut chicken in dice, mix all together with mayonnaise. Serve on hearts of lettuce.

The Public Welfare Department embraced every phase of humanitarian and philanthropic effort, particularly for children. Members sponsored an Atlanta Woman's Club Girl Scout troop, and, continuing their tradition of working for children's health, featured an ongoing annual "Baby Week." In both 1922 and 1923, over 1,000 babies were examined during the one-week enterprise. As a result, permanent health centers were established in every section of the city for mothers to take their babies for examination. The department was also responsible for arranging Christmas trees for special classes in fifteen public schools and giving the Club's annual reception for public school teachers. The club as a whole promoted fair treatment of youth through their support of the opening of a new juvenile detention home.[186]

The Hospital Committee of the Atlanta Woman's Club was responsible for tremendous outreach, not only by giving support in donations, but also in making visits to public hospitals and jails. Each month a program was conducted for disabled veterans. Other outreach projects of this period included the inauguration of "Poppy Day" for the American Legion; conducting the Christmas Seal Sale for the Anti-Tuberculosis Association; providing assistance for the Red Cross and Salvation Army; supporting opportunity schools for foreigners and the disadvantaged; continuing advocacy for better films, good roads, and increased teacher salaries; calling for additional public schools; and, as always, buying Georgia products. Clubwomen were especially concerned with care for the mentally ill, those confined within their community, and those at Milledgeville's Central State Hospital, an institution they considered totally inadequate. Other areas of work included efforts on behalf of the Atlanta Humane Society and protests against the exhibition of trained animals.[187]

The activities of the Atlanta Woman's Club were numerous and far-reaching. Although the organization was and remains nonpolitical, there was no political situation or movement for civic improvement, concerning the welfare of Atlanta, in which the clubwomen did not take part. Eager to learn, especially about new technology, Club members sponsored a program in which the district manager for Southern Bell spoke on issues concerning the telephone and provided demonstrations related to switchboard operation.[188]

186 Atlanta Woman's Club Souvenir Yearbook 1922–1923, p. 15–18, MSS 326–60, Kenan Research Center, Atlanta History Center, Atlanta GA; 1921–1922 Scrapbook, Wimbish House Archives; Boykin, "President's Address," Florence Barnard, pp. 8–10, *Atlanta Woman's Club Yearbook, 1921–1922,* Wimbish House Archives.

187 Atlanta Woman's Club Souvenir Yearbook 1922–1923, pp. 15-18, MSS 326–60, folder box, Kenan Research Center, Atlanta History Center; "Woman's Club Scrapbook, Beginning 1921," Atlanta Woman's Club, Wimbish House Archives, 1921–1922 scrapbook.

188 Atlanta Woman's Club Souvenir Yearbook, p. 20; 1921–1922 scrapbook.

189 Ibid.

190 Ibid., p. 15.

191 "Timeline 2010," Women's History and Resource Center, General Federation of Women's Clubs, Washington, DC; Houde, *Reaching Out: A Story of the General Federation of Women's Clubs* (Washington/Chicago: Mobium Press, 1989) 171–74.

192 Women's Club Scrapbook, beginning 1921, p. 108. AWC Wimbish House Archives; Roth, *Matronage: Patterns In Women's Organizations, Atlanta, Georgia, 1890–1940* (Brooklyn NY: Carlson Publishing, 1994) 37.

193 Atlanta Woman's Club Souvenir Yearbook, p. 19, MSS 326-60, Folder Box Kenan Research Center, Atlanta History Center.

194 Woman's Club Scrapbook, beginning 1921.

The feature program of the Atlanta Woman's Club's 1922–1923 year included a presentation by Dr. E. C. Brooks, a speaker, author, and superintendent of Public Instruction in North Carolina, who was one of America's leading educators. He spoke on the "Essential Factors in Building School Systems." The event, honoring "Education Week," included a welcome given by Atlanta Mayor James L. Key and a performance by the Atlanta Woman's Orchestra, led by Mrs. Annie Munger Mueller.[189]

The clubwomen never faltered in their efforts for Tallulah Falls School or in awarding scholarships to deserving students. By the mid-1920s, hundreds of Georgia's boys and girls had been placed in schools and colleges through scholarships secured by the Atlanta Woman's Club, and the Club was a strong factor in the state's educational development. The Club cooperated with Atlanta's superintendent of education and with the State Department of Education in its many community endeavors.[190]

These early years of the twenties marked major changes for the Atlanta Woman's Club and the General Federation. In 1922, the GFWC purchased 1734 N Street NW in Washington, DC, for its headquarters, and during the Biennial in Chautauqua, New York, it established a Junior Membership Committee. Involving younger members was not a new idea, but the committee formulated goals and made it a priority. Over time, the makeup, ages, and requirements of Junior Clubs would change, but they were fast becoming an integral part of Federation work.[191]

Throughout this time, the Atlanta Woman's Club maintained involvement with ongoing projects, including the Southeastern Fair. The fair was held annually in Atlanta by the Southeastern Fair Association, and at the turn of the century the management of women's activities had been turned over to the Georgia Federation. Under the direction of Atlanta Woman's Club member Nellie Peters Black, who was president of the GaFWC and a member of the Southeastern Fair Association's Women's Committee, the event had included a series of local agricultural fairs and rallies. Attendance had peaked prior to World War I, but interest remained strong. Entries from Atlanta-area women generally included canned, preserved, and baked goods and an assortment of needlework. Writer Jane Anne Settle, now in her 80's, of Jackson, Georgia, was one of thousands of Georgia children who visited the fair as a child. She remembers the event as "an introduction to the 'Big Time,' providing 'little girl' memories still vivid today."[192]

The Club's Hospitality Committee's duties included giving "the glad hand" of fellowship to Club members, meeting and conveying distinguished guests and speakers, and assisting with large receptions. One of the largest and most important of the receptions was the annual event given for state legislators and their wives.[193]

Club programs focused on politics, art, music, literature, education, and other subjects. Discussions ranged from everyday affairs to moral dilemmas, one example being "Is Murder Ever Justified?" Members sponsored special events such as Easter egg hunts, exhibits, art classes, dances, and bridge parties. The women also enjoyed leisure activities.[194]

As the century progressed, the women took greater interest in politics. In one endeavor, they requested representation on a traffic committee study force. The resolution was passed after a discussion of "the difficulties encountered by women automobilists subjected to strictly manmade parking laws." Club member Mrs. Alonzo Richardson asserted the laws were "formulated without reference to that part of Atlanta citizenry which does nine-tenths of the shopping, and has become educated to the virtue of the cash and carry system."[195]

Also during this period, Rebecca Latimer Felton, the nation's first female senator, was the keynote speaker at an Atlanta Woman's Club gathering. She spoke on the value of organized clubwomen to their community, their nation, and the world, and she gave tribute to the Atlanta Woman's Club members and the new auditorium. Following Mrs. Felton's speech, a progression of women including Mrs. Ida Clyde Clarke, Mrs. Rose V. S. Berry, Mrs H. R. Reynolds, and Mrs. W. B. Bomfils (known as author Winnifred Black) presented their views on women's progress. Mrs. Clarke claimed women invented the art of advertising because "Eve's first adventure into publicity oversold to Adam an article he didn't know he needed." Mrs. Bomfils stated, "I belong to 42 clubs and each one is a big affair, but only one club in the world, and that one is in London, equals the Atlanta Woman's Club in achievements and perfection of establishment." AWC president Mrs. Basil Manly Boykin presided over the event during which $3,000 was collected to be applied to the construction of the Club's new banquet hall.[196]

In 1923, the banquet hall was completed at a cost of between $35,000 and $43,000. The facility soon became a venue for dinners, lunches, and other club events and provided a resource for additional revenue. Designed in the style of Louis XV, the hall was appointed with hardwood floors and arched, paneled windows and doors and decorated with French Baroque cupids and a frieze of hand-pressed dentil molding. A hallway connected the banquet hall to the main building and, later, the auditorium. Having a seating capacity of 400, the hall was able to accommodate large card parties, luncheons, receptions, and other social occasions for which the Club was famous.

The Wimbish House, auditorium-theatre, and banquet hall were assets that soon made the Atlanta Woman's Club the clearinghouse for activities reaching into all areas of city life. The three units were surrounded by an exquisite garden filled with a stately water oak, fountain, shrubs, flowers, and layered walks. However, the real work of the Club was centered in the Wimbish House, which contained the office of the executive secretary; president's office; art gallery; co-operative exchange booth; committee rooms; and apartments for the club hostess, club cateress, and salaried employees who resided at the Club.

At the time, the Atlanta Woman's Club held the only art gallery in the city. The gallery displayed works of students and aspiring local artists, as well as many of America's finest artists. Among the most famous were Nicholas R. Brewer, Wilbur Kurtz, and Edgar Nye. The Club, soon known as "the largest and finest in the General Federation of Women's Clubs," was a popular place for women to gather, including Margaret Mitchell, noted author of *Gone With The Wind*.[197]

In May 1923, the Atlanta Woman's Club entertained the Biennial Council of the General Federation of Women's Clubs, thereby gaining the honor of being the first single organization to act as hostess to the General Federation. This was a land-

195 Ibid.

196 Unidentified clipping, in Wimbish House Archives; Staman, *Loosening Corsets* (Macon GA: Tiger Iron Press, 2006) 193–94.

197 Atlanta Woman's Club History #1, Atlanta Woman's Club Collection, Wimbish House Archives; Atlanta Woman's Club Souvenir Book, pp. 7–9; Atlanta Woman's Club Bulletin, 1922; 1895 scrapbook, *Atlanta Woman's Club Scrapbook Collection*, MSS 326–60, Kenan Research Center; Bryant, "History of the Atlanta Woman's Club," typed notes, Atlanta Woman's Club Archives; unidentified clipping, Wimbish House Archives; Atlanta Woman's Club Souvenir Book, 1922–1923, pp. 7–10, MSS 326–60; Sapero, "Atlanta Woman's Club," Wimbish House Archives.

198 "History of the Atlanta Woman's Club: Its Growth and Resultful Achievements," Atlanta Woman's Club Souvenir Book, pp. 3–7, Wimbish House Archives; Atlanta Woman's Club Souvenir Book, 1922–1923, p. 10, MSS 326–60.

199 "Mr. Jackson Voices Ideals of American Homes At Woman's Club" *Atlanta Journal*, 13 Nov 1923, p. 20, Wimbish House Archives.

200 1921 scrapbook, *Atlanta Woman's Club Scrapbook Collection*, p. 159, Wimbish House Archives; 1923–1924 scrapbook, Wimbish House Archives.

201 "The Woman's Club," unidentified article, MSS 353, Scrapbook #18, MSS 326–360, ovz 3.39, Kenan Research Center,.

202 "Atlanta Woman's Club to Sponsor Big Golf Match Wednesday Afternoon at Druid Hills" (16 July 1924), "Woman's Club Event to Have Wide Appeal," and "The Woman's Club," unidentified articles, MSS 353, scrapbook #18, ovz 3.39, Kenan Research Center, Atlanta History Center.

203 Karen Thomson, "President's Message," Atlanta Woman's Club Newsletter, November 2008.

mark for the Club and for Atlanta, which had become known as the "Convention City," ranking second among the cities of the country in the number of conventions it entertained annually. The event was such a spectacular occasion, the Inter-Civic League, the Presidents Club, the American Legion, the United States Army, the City Federation, and every civic organization lent its aid in entertaining the visitors.[198]

Throughout the twenties, club members still stood firm on their emphasis of tying women's roles to their homes. "Woman and the Home" was the subject of a program by Marion M. Jackson, a prominent attorney and civic leader: "His address was an earnest plea for the preservation of the ideal American home" as he called attention to the plight of rural women and the help that could be given by those who were "more cultured." He placed the responsibility of maintaining a happy and successful home squarely on the shoulders of the women: "Out of every ten marriages, there is one which ends in divorce, and if the day ever comes when man looks to woman for the ideal and finds nothing but the material, what will become of the world then? In God's name, women, teach the little girls to sustain civilization."[199]

Amazingly, by 1923, the Atlanta Woman's Club had over 1,200 members. Their community, General Federation, and State Federation work continued, as did their projects such as work at the municipal market, book donations to library extension programs, and assistance for the Parent-Teacher Association and schools. They also supported the Community House for girls, as well as Grady and other hospitals, and they continued their work in the areas of criminal justice, juvenile justice, reducing the crime rate, improving the prison system, and advocating for prisoners' vocational education. They were especially concerned with issues related to pollution, drug abuse, and murder committed by minors.[200]

In praise of the Atlanta Woman's Club, a local paper stated, "It is timely to commend the magnificent work that the Atlanta Woman's Club is doing in all worth-while undertakings of a cultural and civic nature. The home of the Club, with its magnificent auditorium, is one of the finest and most spacious in the United States. The Club itself is institutional. Under the roof of this beautiful building, sponsored by this parent organization, are concentrated women's activities touching every phase of citizenship, community service, and the advancement and uplifting of all people, morally, educationally, and culturally. Atlantans should never stint in their encouragement to this remarkable organization that means so much to Atlanta and the higher ideals of her people."[201]

During 1924, the Atlanta Woman's Club sponsored a golf tournament at Druid Hills featuring some of the most outstanding golfers in the world. Among the players were national champion Bobby Jones, Southern champion Perry Adair, and other stars such as Tom Prescott and Charley Black. The four eminent players were honored by the Atlanta Woman's Club executive board at a Wimbish House luncheon.[202] Another outstanding event of that year was the appearance of Houdini, who gave a lecture in the new auditorium.[203]

Also in 1924, after noting that the Piedmont Driving Club had a swimming pool that was revenue producing, the clubwomen decided to build their own pool. The next year, just to the south of the auditorium, a fine rectangular swimming pool was installed with easy access to the dressing rooms under the auditorium stage. The pool was built by C. R. Justi under the direction of the Case and Company Architectural Firm and named for Deryl H. Sharp. Members were allowed to swim for a nominal fee.[204]

These Club projects, constructed with the highest quality of designs and materials, served to enhance the beauty of this eclectic venue, affording the opportunity for a wide variety of programs and services: "The Wimbish House became a focal point for civic and social events, with a catering department, hosting many of Atlanta and the Nation's most prominent citizens. Over time, its guests have included four United States first ladies, as well as political leaders, diplomats, screen stars and famous musicians, authors, and speakers. One of the first women to receive an honorary life membership in the Atlanta Woman's Club was Mrs. Franklin Delano (Eleanor) Roosevelt."[205]

Also in 1924, the Atlanta Woman's Club planted elm and crepe myrtle trees along the thoroughfares and in what is now the Woodrow Wilson Monument Park, located at the intersection of Morningside Drive and Rock Springs Road. Their planting was dedicated as a living memorial to Woodrow Wilson in honor of his leadership during World War I and as an advocate of permanent world peace through the League of Nations.[206]

Meanwhile, the new and improved Atlanta Municipal Market opened with fanfare, immediately attracting a large number of farmers and an even larger number of eager customers. The Atlanta Woman's Club celebrated its success as did other contributing organizations: "The curb market concept had begun with the Atlanta Woman's Club, Atlanta Federation of Woman's Clubs, city and county public school systems, and black educational institutions' promotion of gardening activities." It had been Mrs. Norman Sharp and the Atlanta Woman's Club market committee who had served as the final impetus to establishing the market.[207]

Continuing to enjoy a wide variety of educational programs, in early 1925, the Atlanta Woman's Club invited two of the world's most recognized pilots, Lieutenants Jack Harding and Lowell Thomas, to speak about the potential of the "Air Age." And speak they did: "The air—the air, that's the big thing of the future. Wars of the future, if there are wars, will be fought there, and perhaps peace preserved there," said one lieutenant.[208]

Because of the city's reliance on rail, the pilots had to take a train. The clubwomen, realizing that Atlanta was lagging behind other urban centers, became convinced the city would not thrive without building an airport. Adamant in this belief, they convinced Atlanta mayor Walter Sims, who in turn convinced Councilman William B. Hartsfield, that the time was at hand for Atlanta to enter the "Age of Air."

In February 1925, a committee of twenty Atlanta Woman's Club members called on Mayor Sims and urged him to have the city purchase a landing field. Mayor Sims appointed Atlanta Woman's Club president Mrs. Norman Sharp to be a member of the City Landing Field Committee. She was later elected first vice president of the Atlanta Chapter of the National Aeronautical Association. Thus began the chain of events leading to the development of the Atlanta airport, with air service beginning at Candler Field in May 1928.[209]

204 Mrs. Curtis H. Bryant, "History of the Atlanta Woman's Club," collection, Wimbish House Archives; 1924 scrapbook, Wimbish House Archives; "Atlanta Woman's Club History #1" and Atlanta Woman's Club Bulletin, 1922, Atlanta Woman's Club, Wimbish House Archives; "Atlanta Woman's Club Scrapbooks Collection," Finding Aid MSS 326–60, Kenan Research Center, Atlanta History Center.

205 "Atlanta Woman's Club History #1"; "The Atlanta Woman's Club Celebrates 100 Years," *Northside Neighbor*, section B, p. 2, 8 November 1995, Wimbish House Archives.

206 Lisa Banes, email to Anne B. Jones, 8 March 2010.

207 Boutwell, "The Sweet Spot: Sweet Auburn Curb Market Is an Atlanta Institution," *Intown-Buckhead-North Community*, unidentified clipping, Wimbish House Archives.

208 Unidentified article, *The Atlanta Georgian*, 3 Mar 1925, Wimbish House Archives; *Business to Business*, pp. 127–28, in Wimbish House Archives; letter from Atlanta Woman's Club board of trustees member Elizabeth M. Burris to Lee Morris, city council member, 4 Feb 2000, Wimbish House Archives.

209 "Atlanta Woman's Club History #1," Wimbish House Archives; Atlanta Woman's Club Biennial Report—1966–1968, p.48, MSS 353; Blass, Kimberly S., and Rose, Michael, *Images of Atlanta: Atlanta Scenes*, Photojournalism in the Atlanta History Center Collection, p. 30, fig. 294.A857 A876, Arcadia Publishing 1998.

210 Ibid., 59.

211 "Atlanta Woman's Club History #1"; Atlanta Woman's Club Biennial Report—1966–1968, p. 48, MSS 353.

212 "Atlanta Woman's Club History #1"; "Atlanta Woman's Club Celebrates 100 Years," *Northside Neighbor*, B2; flyer, Atlanta Woman's Club's Wimbish House Archives.

213 Wifford, William Bailey, "Up from Boarding House Row," p. 149, *Peachtree Street, Atlanta*, loose pages, Wimbish House Archives; "From a Vision to a Successful Achievement," unidentified article, Wimbish House Archives.

By the early 1940s, Atlanta's airport had become one of the busiest. It was also "the first to have an air traffic control and instrument approach system." In 1961, the city celebrated the opening of its new airport building, "the largest single terminal in the country," signaling Atlanta's entry into the "Jet Age."[210] Atlanta's Municipal Airport, renamed Hartsfield-Jackson Atlanta International Airport in the first decade of the twenty-first century, earned the distinction of being the busiest airport in the world.[211]

Also in 1925, clubwomen planted forty water oaks in Piedmont Park, calling them the "Mayor's Memory Grove" in honor of each of Atlanta's former mayors. Atlanta's Grand Dames installed an accompanying marker, made of granite from Stone Mountain Park, that was engraved with each mayor's name. Today, as each mayor leaves office, his or her name is added to the roster. The Club's Conservation Program also sponsored the planting of a thousand flowering peach trees along Peachtree Street from North Avenue to Oglethorpe University. The Club has continued supporting Atlanta tree-planting projects to the present day.[212]

In 1926, the Atlanta Woman's Club further extended its tree-planting projects, prevailing upon the developers of Morningside to beautify Morningside Drive. The clubwomen appealed to the owners of the property to plant 3 elm trees and 3 crepe myrtles every 100 feet on both sides of the street. The elm was chosen because it lives and grows for generations, maturing within a short span of years. The trees would create a beautiful arch under which one could pass for a distance of over 2 miles. The planting was again a tribute, this time to the "great statesman" Woodrow Wilson. In addition, a small, beautiful park between Morningside Drive and Rock Springs Road was turned over to the Club for the erection of a bronze table, supported by a granite base, with an inscription telling of the achievements of the man they considered the world's greatest statesman. That same year, the Club was the site of the formation of the Atlanta Historical Society. The organization grew, attracting scholars and other interested members, and eventually evolved into one of the most respected historical societies in the nation. Members gradually

Mrs. B. M. Boykin
1921–1923

Mrs. Alonzo Richardson
1923–1924

Mrs. Norman Sharp
1924–1926

Mrs. Price Smith
1926–1928

Mrs. Charles Goodman
May 1928–January 1929

Mrs. John R. Hornaday
January 1929–May 1930

amassed a large collection of old records, books, pictures, and artifacts, which are presently housed in the Atlanta History Center.[213]

By 1927, Atlanta's Municipal Market included sixty stalls, some the size of a store, selling thousands of pounds of produce. It was well on its way to becoming an Atlanta institution.[214]

From 1928 to 1929, the Atlanta Woman's Club's presidency underwent a period of confusion. Official records now list Mrs. Charles Goodman as president from May 1928 to January 1929 and Mrs. John R. Hornady as president for the last six months remaining of the annual term until she was elected to a full one-year term. The distraction was short-lived and the Club was soon back on track, serving its burgeoning membership as well as the local community.[215]

While the Atlanta Woman's Club was expanding, so was Tallulah Falls Industrial School. In 1920, the state school superintendent advised the separation of the public school at Tallulah Falls from Tallulah Falls Industrial School, but many in Rabun County continued to send their children to Tallulah Falls Industrial School for a small tuition fee of approximately a dollar per child per year.

The school continued its academic program and also supported the state Federation's emphasis on promoting the teaching and selling of Georgia crafts.

In 1925, the Atlanta Federation Schoolhouse and Isma Dooley Auditorium were dedicated. Mrs. Dooley, a journalist for the *Atlanta Constitution*, was one of the founders of the Atlanta Woman's Club. A "Greater Tallulah" fundraising campaign resulted in a new campus water supply and a new swimming pool and, by 1929, the school's grounds included 250 acres of land with 11 buildings. Eleven accredited grades served 265 students, and the school had $80,000 of invested funds.[216]

The greatest accomplishment of this period occurred when the Georgia legislature finally passed the Child Labor Bill. Because of the intense work Georgia's clubwomen invested to promote the bill, Governor Clifford Walker presented the pen used to sign the bill to the Georgia Federation of Women's Clubs. Georgia, under the influence of the interests of powerful industrial forces, "was the last state to

214 Ann Taylor Boutwell, "The Sweet Spot," *Intown-Buckhead-North Community.*

215 Wifford, "Up from Boarding House Row," pp. 130–31.

216 "Celebrating 100 Years of Excellence," *Tallulah Falls School Magazine* 30/3 (Fall 2008) p. 24, Wimbish House Archives; Hancock, *Not By Magic: But By Faith, Courage and Earnest Work* (Toccoa GA: Commercial Printing Company, 1982) 25.

217 "GaFWC History," GFWC/Georgia Federation of Women's Clubs, www.gafwc.org/html/gafwc_history.johnson.html.

218 "President's List," Atlanta Woman's Club, Wimbish House Archives.

protect children with a Child Labor Law." Other work that had come to fruition was members' push for the establishment of reformatories later called Georgia Training Centers for Boys.[217]

Atlanta Woman's Club presidents during this challenging period were Mrs. B. M. Boykin (1921–1923), Mrs. Alonzo Richardson (1923–1924), Mrs. Norman Sharp (1924–1926), Mrs. Price Smith (1926–1928), Mrs. Charles Goodman (May 1928–January 1929) and Mrs. John R. Hornaday (January 1929–May 1930).[218]

CHAPTER FOURTEEN

When Hitler crosses swords with the women of America, he will meet his Waterloo.

Sara A. Whitehurst[219]
President, GFWC

he United States entered the decade of the 1930s in financial panic as the speculation of the 1920s caught up with reality, resulting in the Great Depression. Banks failed, stock prices plummeted, and unemployment figures soared. The Atlanta Woman's Club, the Georgia Federation of Women's Clubs (GaFWC), and the General Federation of Women's Clubs (GFWC) were concerned with the cost of club work as well as members' own financial conditions. Holding conventions, maintaining clubhouses, printing magazines, and paying membership dues became challenging as did members' continuing efforts to help those in need. Economic problems affected every area of activity as clubs struggled to save and provide stability for their ongoing local projects.[220]

The GFWC emphasized thrift as a practice helpful to individuals and the nation as members worked to prevent the loss of the progressive steps they had made and to support their communities. Clubs responded to the crisis with a wide variety of humanitarian acts and service efforts. Concerned about the loss of programs due to economic stress, they began Penny Art Funds to support local artists; these Penny Art Funds continue today. Noting a mass exodus of farmers to the north and to cities, Georgia clubwomen intensified their Georgia products support, leading a statewide movement to widen the outlet for Georgia farm goods. Working with the

219 Houde, *Reaching Out: A Story of the General Federation of Women's Clubs* (Washington/Chicago: Mobium Press, 1989) 239.

220 Ibid., 191–93; Atlanta Woman's Club Biennial Report—1966–1968, p.49, MSS 353, Kenan Research Center, Atlanta History Center, Atlanta GA.

221 Houde, *Reaching Out*, 193–205; Mrs. Clyde F. Anderson, ed., "A Walk through History—Georgia Federation of Women's Clubs 1896–1986," paper, Wimbish House Archives, Atlanta GA.

222 Ibid.; Houde, *Reaching Out*, 193–205.

223 *Annual Report of Atlanta Woman's Club, 1930–31*, p. 56, courtesy of Daisy Luckey Aukerman's Woman's Club Archives, personal collection.

224 Anderson, ed., "A Walk through History."

225 Houde, *Reaching Out*, 193–205; "Timeline 2010," Women's History and Resource Center, General Federation of Women's Clubs, Washington DC.

226 Houde, *Reaching Out*, 212–22; Anderson, ed., "A Walk through History."

227 *Annual Report of Atlanta Woman's Club*, 37–44.

Georgia Federation, Club members staged "An exposition of Georgia-grown and Georgia-made products at the Atlanta City Auditorium."[221]

Throughout the General Federation, members became increasingly concerned with issues related to global problems and international relations. They also continued their national and local support of programs to prevent crime, reform prisons, fight illiteracy, and halt the proliferation of drug abuse.[222]

During the spring of 1931, the Garden Division of the Atlanta Woman's Club sponsored plant sales at the Farmers' Market to help women from rural areas learn about native plants, promote their conservation, and encourage their sales as an additional source of income. The endeavor put rural farmers in touch with Atlantans and helped increase profits for the market in general.[223]

Meanwhile, the Georgia Federation stressed the need for educational presentations related to family finance and home projects, and the clubwomen continued to hold and attend programs on self-improvement. [224]

As the Great Depression continued, the women witnessed increasing unemployment, foreclosures, bankruptcies, and business closings. On the national level, General Federation of Women's Club members continued their attempts to elevate and improve the status of all women, including those who remained at home. The organization led a nationwide survey on household technology and produced a five-part Home Equipment Primer to educate families on using available utilities to maximize labor saving. Their campaign would eventually result in "homemaker" being included as an identified occupation for the first time in the 1930 United States census.[225]

At the same time the women were awed by the number of new labor-saving appliances, they were also aware that women were bearing more responsibility for supplementing family incomes and, in some cases, providing it all. As the nation entered the New Deal, the issue of more women entering the workforce without usurping the men and women who already depended on these jobs became a matter of grave concern.[226]

Despite so many crises and concerns, the Atlanta Woman's Club's Fine Arts Division continued to present outstanding entertainment programs, one of which included living models representing famous pieces of sculpture, "some of which came to life and danced." Honored guests were the Sculptors of Atlanta and several prominent artists. Local dancing schools were involved in the program, after which guests viewed a collection of sculpture. Club members engaged in numerous fundraising enterprises, such as a cooperative effort with Rich's department store to present a "cotton fashion show" in which members modeled clothing. AWC members obtained and awarded scholarships in academics, music, drama, dancing, and secretarial work; participated in jail visitation; helped the unemployed; assisted the needy; promoted juvenile justice; and, of course, donated substantial sums to Tallulah Falls School. Other efforts included working with the Atlanta Better Films Committee, giving help to the blind, supporting the arts, and paying rent for people without means.[227]

Crime remained in the spotlight as members became increasingly concerned about safety in their local communities. Discontent was rampant as citizens blamed the government for lack of jobs, financial losses, and economic insecurity. Families, stricken by the precarious situation, listened intently to news broadcasts from their living room radios. In 1933, the General Federation, realizing the need to reach these families, began weekly radio broadcasts in cooperation with the Consumers' Counsel of the Department of Agriculture. The series was presented as a public service program from the National Broadcasting Company.

Clubwomen followed the GFWC initiative of emphasizing the importance of budgeting and thrift as they continued their support of local reading and library projects. Historically, their efforts were so fervent that the American Library Association credited General Federation clubs with having established 75 percent of the nation's libraries.[228]

Cancer was an area of growing alarm as the women attempted to work with the American Cancer Society to "fight fear and dispel the ignorance of the dreaded disease" while giving special attention to early diagnosis and treatment. Other worrisome issues involved automotive safety and the need for many homemakers to find ways of generating cash for their families' survival. Community concerns included the growing use of billboards on Georgia's streets and highways and, as was thought by many, the unhealthiness and immorality of "Marathon Dances." As they had in the past, local and national club members continued their focus on child labor, state and national parks, and forestry. They also continued to work for the rights and economic elevation of Native Americans.[229]

On the positive side, the Atlanta Woman's Club and others celebrated the finalization of their efforts for women to be admitted to the University of Georgia and their inclusion as physicians at the State Hospital for the mentally ill. The Georgia clubwomen's longtime interest in preservation and protecting the state's natural resources resulted in the creation of both Neal Gap Forest Park and Indian Springs Forest Park. Indian Springs is the nation's oldest state park.[230]

By this time, Junior Clubs were becoming an increasingly vital part of the Georgia and General Federations. Clubwomen realized the importance of grooming younger generations to continue their local, state, national, and global efforts. In 1934, Mrs. John F. MacDougald organized the Junior Atlanta Woman's Club. It was considered a part of the Atlanta Woman's Club and became an official Federation club the following year. The Club followed the AWC in its support for charities, the arts, and education. [231]

As harsh economic times continued, clubwomen all over the United States became worried about international concerns, particularly ideological conflicts threatening democracy and peace. Club members all over the United States embarked on endeavors to raise international consciousness through learning and forming relationships with women in other countries. Meanwhile, they continued their "home" projects. The Atlanta Woman's Club, along with other Fifth District clubs, set a goal of planting a million dogwood trees in Fulton, DeKalb, and Rockdale counties by 1940.[232]

Tallulah Falls School continued to grow. The word "Industrial" was eventually taken out of the school's name as it continued its academic program, but it became known for supporting and promoting the teaching and selling of Georgia crafts. The

228 Houde, *Reaching Out*, 204–206; "Timeline 2010."

229 Houde, *Reaching Out*, 206–222; Anderson, ed., "A Walk through History."

230 Ibid.

231 "Atlanta Woman's Club History #1," paper, Wimbish House Archives; Anderson, ed., "A Walk through History"; "History: Junior Atlanta Woman's Club," 1950–1951 Yearbook of the Junior Atlanta Woman's Club, p. 7, MSS 353, Kenan Research Center.

232 Houde, *Reaching Out*, 219–20; Anderson, ed., "A Walk through History"; "Atlanta Woman's Club History #1."

233 "Celebrating 100 Years of Excellence," *Tallulah Falls School Magazine* 30/3 (Fall 2008): 26, in Wimbish House Archives; Hancock, *Not By Magic: But By Faith, Courage and Earnest Work* (Toccoa GA: Commercial Printing Company, 1982) 59.

234 Atlanta Woman's Club Biennial Report—1966–1968, p. 49, MSS 353, Kenan Research Center; Anderson, ed., "A Walk through History"; Atlanta Woman's Club History #1.

235 Biennial Report–Atlanta Woman's Club, 1935–1937, pp. 14–18, MSS 353.

236 Georgia Federation of Women's Clubs, 5th District Records, Yearbook 1935–1936, pp. 68–71, Georgia Archives, box 4, accn. 1975 0487M, Morrow GA.

237 Anderson, ed., "A Walk through History."

school was soon famous throughout the country for its outstanding work in basketry, rugs, spreads, and pottery.[233] Still, the economy worsened. Thrown into the melee were the growing problems of alcohol and drug abuse, which undermined the welfare of the very groups members wanted to help. At the 1930 General Federation Convention in Denver, Federation members had endorsed Prohibition. Under AWC president Mrs. Max E. Land's direction (1933–1935), these issues became even more pressing. After reviewing a report giving statistics on the amounts and kinds of narcotics being sold in Atlanta and the state, members began outlining plans to eliminate them.[234]

In 1935, when President Roosevelt visited the state, Atlanta Woman's Club president Mrs. Wightman F. Melton (1935–1937) served on Georgia's Welcoming Committee. By this time, the Club had become a meeting place, exhibition site, and support venue for all forms of the arts, including the Atlanta Writers Club, which held monthly dinners in the banquet hall.[235]

According to the 1935–1936 Georgia Federation Yearbook, the dogwood planting project of the Georgia Federation's Fifth District gained much political and local attention. Atlanta mayor James L. Key formed a committee to look into extending the project throughout Atlanta, involving the public and all civic organizations. Mrs. Paul J. McGovern became chairman of the committee and a plan was presented whereby the eventual 1 million dogwood trees could be secured. The US Forestry Service, Civilian Conservation Corps, Public Works Administration, and Atlanta city council assisted in the effort, with the city council agreeing to provide burlap and other essential items.

In spring 1936, 12,500 trees were planted without any cost to the city; an equal number were ready to be planted in the fall. The rest of the trees were to be planted over a period of five years. "The campaign resulted in the first Arbor Day Tree Inspection Motorcade, conducted by the district, with the Atlanta Woman's Club acting as chairman. Thirty cars full of clubwomen participated in this unique venture." Among the clubwomen's other efforts during this period were furnishing food, toys, clothing, and other necessities for needy families at Christmas and presenting noteworthy exhibits and prominent speakers for public enjoyment. Newspapers cited the Atlanta Woman's Club as being "most active in community service, cooperating in patriotic meetings and drives."[236]

The year 1937 was a landmark year for the Georgia Federation (GaFWC). The Georgia legislature finally passed legislation that would provide free textbooks for Georgia schoolchildren and require drivers' licenses to operate motor vehicles. For years clubwomen had advocated for the passage of these bills.[237]

In the late 1930s, the Atlanta Woman's Club joined with the GaFWC in emphasizing help for Georgia's faltering economy. Noting the continuing mass exodus of farmers to the north and to cities, Federation members led a statewide movement to widen the outlet for Georgia farm goods, including "An exposition of Georgia-grown and Georgia-made products staged by clubwomen at the Atlanta City Auditorium."[238]

During this era, Atlanta Woman's Club member Mrs. John K. Ottley used her power and influence to secure the construction of a bridge across Tallulah Gorge. The bridge, named in her honor, made a major impact on the region, creating a surge

Mrs. Thornton Fincher
1930–1931

Mrs. William P. Dunn
1931–1933

Mrs. Max Land
1933–1935

in economic growth. Another highlight of the 1930s was the appearance of actress Tallulah Bankhead as guest at an Atlanta Woman's Club meeting.[239]

The Atlanta Woman's Club continued to promote programs and activities in the areas of art, citizenship, gardening, bridge, highway beautification, crafts, health and welfare, needlework, legislative issues, and scholarships. Members sponsored boys clubs, girls clubs, and the city's food market and hall; they also worked with the Red Cross to make bandages and clothes for the needy.[240]

During the 1939–1940 club year, members held classes and divisional meetings on such diverse subjects as amateur writing, art design, book reviews, bridge, gardening, interior decorating, music, public speaking, furniture finishing, and Red Cross sewing. One of the most popular offerings was a "book exchange." The Georgia Writers division provided the Club with access to presentations from notable Georgia writers and set aside an annual Georgia Writers Day. The International Relations Department tackled concerns related to war, fear, and propaganda, attempting to teach community members "to distinguish fact from propaganda, to keep idealism free from ignorance, to preserve individually a sense of justice and tolerance, and as a group to aid in the cause of peace and liberty for all people." Another endeavor was the formation of a Speakers Bureau to present informative programs to community organizations and groups.[241]

The Public Welfare Department maintained a room at the Wimbish House for the storage of donated items for the city's needy and, as a fundraiser, presented an enactment of *The Bridal Chorus*. The comedy was performed in the auditorium with a cast of members from the Atlanta Theatre Guild. For their 1939 birthday celebration, Atlanta Woman's Club members produced *The Court of Public Opinion*, an historical play based on the Club's history.[242]

"Purely a charitable enterprise" from its inception, the Atlanta Woman's Club sought to fill gaps not covered by other organizations and agencies, and it found the broad scope of its endeavors as limitless as "woman's work which never ends." Because of the large size of its membership, the many necessary

238 Ibid.

239 Ibid.; Atlanta Woman's Club History #1; Sapero, "Atlanta Woman's Club," Wimbish House Archives.

240 Atlanta Woman's Club #1.

241 Atlanta Woman's Club Bulletin: 1939–1940, pp. 19–33, Wimbish House Archives.

242 Ibid., 33.

243 "Atlanta Woman's Club vs. City of Atlanta, and J. Ben Daniel Marshall," no. 88, 684, Fulton Superior Court Injunction, 23 April 1931, in *Annual Report of Atlanta Woman's Club*, 1930–31, Daisy Luckey Aukerman's Woman's Club Archives, personal collection.

244 Atlanta Woman's Club Biennial Report—1966–1968, p.49, MSS 353.

committees, and the need for adequate space to present programs designed to educate its members, the AWC required spacious quarters. In the 1930s, the Club struggled to balance the need for revenue to accomplish its good works and maintain its facilities with the challenges of ever-increasing taxation. This issue is as important to members today as it was then, but it was especially difficult during the years of the Great Depression.[243]

Leading the women through these seemingly insurmountable times were Mrs. Thornton Fincher (1930–1931), Mrs. William P. Dunn (1931–1933), Mrs. Max Land ((1933–1935), Mrs. Wightman F. Melton (1935–1937), Mrs. Alva Maxwell (1937–1939), and Mrs. Calvin Shelverton (1939–1940). During the presidency of Mrs. William P. Dunn, Eleanor Roosevelt was elected honorary member and was "very happy to accept."[244]

Mrs. Wightman F. Melton
1935-1937

Mrs. Alva Maxwell
1937-1939

Mrs. Calvin Shelverton
1939-1940

CHAPTER FIFTEEN

*I believe that the American woman, through control of a large share
of the family budget, exerts a vital influence upon today's economic
order.*

Mrs. Clarence Fraim[245]
Excerpt from GFWC "Shopper's Creed"

The year 1940 marked the fiftieth anniversary of the General Federation of Women's Clubs, and clubs everywhere participated in the Jubilee Celebration. The organization had grown to 15,000 clubs with more than 2 million members. As members rejoiced, they steered their clubs toward emphasizing peace, learning about international affairs, and strengthening the forces of democracy. At the same time, Atlanta Woman's Club members witnessed the world exploding again in conflict. They became increasingly concerned about the escalating war in Europe, the need for a strong national defense, and the provision of materials and resources for those in our country's army camps.

In this time of fear and uncertainty, the General Federation sought to draw members together, encouraging strength through solidarity. GFWC president Sara A. Whitehurst referred clubwomen to the *Collect* written by Mary Stewart in 1904 and used by clubs throughout the country. The *Collect*, with its emphasis on good character and unity, is still used by the Atlanta Woman's Club and other clubs' members today.[246]

245 Mrs. Clarence Fraim, excerpt from GFWC "Shopper's Creed," in Houde, *Reaching Out: A Story of the General Federation of Women's Clubs* (Washington/Chicago: Mobium Press, 1989) 205.

246 Houde, *Reaching Out*, 219–43.

A COLLECT FOR CLUB WOMEN

Keep us, Oh God, from pettiness,
Let us be large in thought, in word, in deed.

Let us be done with fault finding
And leave off self-seeking.

May we put away all pretense
And meet each other face to face.
Without self-pity and without prejudice.

May we never be hasty in judgment,
And always generous.

Let us take time for all things;
Make us to grow calm, serene, gentle.

Teach us to put into action our better impulses,
Straightforward and unafraid.

Grant that we may realize it is the little things that
Create differences.
That in the big things of life we are at one.

And may we strive to touch and to know the great,
Common human heart of us all. And oh, Lord God, let
Us forget not to be kind.

—Mary Stewart, April 1904

Traditionally, the AWC General Meetings have ended with Club members' reading of the Collect. The Atlanta Woman's Club began singing the Collect at the end of each General Meeting in 2009 when AWC President Karen Thomson was given the arrangement, below, by International GFWC President Rose Ditto at the 2009 International GFWC Convention in Cleveland, Ohio. At the 2011 GaFWC Convention at Callaway Gardens, the Collect was sung at the Closing Session:

A COLLECT FOR CLUB WOMEN
(Sung to the tune of *America, the Beautiful*)

Keep us, O God, from pettiness, all finding fault be done.
Let us be large in word and deed, each day from sun to sun.
Help us, fault finding to leave off, self-seeking not to wish.
Let's meet each other face to face without a prejudice.

May hasty judgment be left out, our thoughts be generous.
Make us be gentle, calm, serene, and so industrious.
Grant us that we may realize small things may be ignored,
That all the greater things in life, no difference can afford.

Dear Lord, we ask in earnest prayer that we may strive to know
The common human heart of all, as on through life we go.
Thy help, Dear Lord, we humbly ask, to strive with heart and mind,
In all the work that we may do, let's forget-not-to-be-kind.

Throughout the thirties, Atlanta Woman's Club members had undergone severe financial struggles. During the presidency of Mrs. Howard Pattillo (1941–1943), the clubwomen decided to form a Board of Trustees to guide the Club's business affairs. Helping to maintain economic and membership stability, the Board of Trustees is still in operation and is responsible for the maintenance of the Wimbish House and the rental of its facilities.[247]

On 7 December 1941, the lives of Americans changed forever. With the bombing of Pearl Harbor, clubwomen immediately shifted their efforts from advocating peace to promoting national defense. Rooms on the second floor of the General Federation of Women's Clubs' headquarters in Washington, DC, were converted into war service offices as the Federation began a massive attempt to provide resources for the war effort. Among the GFWC's projects were support and help for service men and women in army camps, nurse recruitments and scholarships, support of the American Red Cross, and the sales of stamps and war bonds.[248]

"Wartime activities included participation in Red Cross war programs, nurses' aide and home nursing courses, wartime nutrition classes, utilization of woman power in industry and in agriculture, salvage and conservation of war products, endorsement of rationing and price controls, victory gardens, and recognition of women on policy-forming committees of government."[249] Federation members also worked on policies for the abolishment of sex discrimination, a project for the provision of bridal gowns for British servicewomen, and affairs of national and international scope.[250]

Realizing that the cost for a heavy bomber could be as much as $300,000, a medium bomber $175,000, and a fighter plane $75,000, club members began participating in a "Buy a Bomber" campaign. Planes were named for state federations, groups of clubs, and individual clubs. Many of our nation's planes carried these names on their noses, including one named "Tallulah." Nationally, the women put forth an astounding effort, with sales totaling $101,617,750. The project was followed by a program to finance an air armada for the Navy, during which $154,459,132 was raised, allowing for the purchase of 431 planes. The Federation's Victory Loan Drive raised $90,794,182.[251]

247 Atlanta Woman's Club Biennial Report—1966–1968, p.49, MSS 353, folder box, Kenan Research Center, Atlanta History Center, Atlanta GA.

248 Houde, *Reaching Out*, 239–46.

249 Ibid.

250 Ibid., 245–56.

251 Ibid.; "Celebrating 100 Years of Excellence," *Tallulah Falls School Magazine* 30/3 (Fall 2008): 27, in Wimbish House Archives, Atlanta GA.

Four AWC women, First and Fiftieth Yearbooks, and what appears to be a newspaper photo of the Women's Building of the Cotton States and International Exposition, Atlanta, Georgia, during the Fall of 1895. Dated May, 1946. From left to right: Mrs. Frank A. Dennis, President of the Georgia Federation of Women's Clubs; Mrs. John F. MacDougald, President of the Atlanta Woman's Club; Mrs. Turner E. Smith, Co-Chairman Scrap Book Exhibit, Georgia Federation Convention May 8-10, 1946 Atlanta Biltmore Hotel; Mrs. R. C. Fryer, Jr., past president of the Georgia Federation and Chairman for the Anniversary Year

252 Anderson, ed., "A Walk through History"; Houde, *Reaching Out*, 263–66.

253 Atlanta Woman's Club Biennial Report—1966–1968, p. 50, MSS 353.

254 "Timeline 2010," Women's History and Resource Center, General Federation of Women's Clubs, Washington DC; unidentified article, *The Atlanta Constitution*, 21 June 1944, accn. 1975–0487M, Georgia Archives, Morrow GA; unidentified article, *The Atlanta Constitution*, 25 July 1944, Finding Aid acct. 1975–0487M, Georgia Archives; Eugenia B. Cordon, "3 Audiences Cheer Rubinoff," *The Atlanta Constitution*, 13 May 1944, 1975–0487M, Georgia Archives.

In 1942, the Atlanta Woman's Club joined other state Federation clubs in donating 568,000 hours in service to defense. In 1944, the General Federation (GFWC) sold $65 million in bonds for a fleet of bombers and Georgia club women sold and purchased almost $2.5 million in bonds. The number of international clubs was growing, as well as an increased world consciousness. This led to the desire for closer ties with other clubwomen of the US and other countries.[252]

The war years took a heavy economic toll on all organizations. The Atlanta Woman's Club, facing a looming financial crisis, rallied to save the Wimbish House and its adjoining buildings from foreclosure. By 1944, their efforts had resulted in refinance of the mortgage and fiscal stability.[253]

Despite their focus on war service and budget concerns, the women continued community and national efforts at home, particularly their support of educational and women's issues. In 1944, the GFWC endorsed the Equal Rights Amendment. Club members supported a local Red Cross chapter at the Club and continued their support of Georgia homemade and home-grown products, joining other women's clubs in hosting Georgia product dinners throughout the state. The Atlanta Woman's Club also continued their support for the arts and other programs, among which was a concert for Russian violinist David Rubinoff and his accompanist Alexander Makofka.[254]

In December, under the direction of the War Service Committee and its chairman Mrs. Ralph McGill, soldiers from Lawson General Hospital and Fort

To celebrate the Club's 50th Birthday, on Nov. 12, 1945, AWC members dramatized the Atlanta Woman's Club Organizational Meeting in 1895 in the play "Golden Years" by AWC member and former president Mrs. Alva G. Maxwell. Members from left to right: Mrs. W. P. Harding, Jr., Mrs. Elmer L. Stanley, Mrs. Clarke Donaldson, Mrs. George Cotsakis, Mrs. W. Beverly Johnson, Mrs. Cecil Kinnett, Mrs. H. W. Gullat, Mrs. J. G. Lee, Mrs. E. E. Nicholson, Mrs. L. W. Stynchcombe, Mrs. E. Wayne West, Mrs. T. L. Hoshall, Jr.

McPherson were guests of the Atlanta Woman's Club during a Christmas party with Santa Claus and gifts. "One hundred debutantes added beauty and gaiety" to the festivities, which included old-fashioned turkey and trimmings, fortune telling, jitterbug dancing, and singing.[255] Sadly, in 1944, fire destroyed the original Willet building at Tallulah Falls School. So devoted were the women that a new structure was completed the following year.[256]

In 1945 the Atlanta Woman's Club's Tallulah Falls Committee sponsored *Personal Appearance*, a delightful three-act comedy presented by the Atlanta Theater Guild for the benefit of the school's building fund. Other featured events included an appearance by Judge William Black, noted author and authority on the League of Nations; the Georgia Tech Glee Club's presentation of the opera *Martha*; a program on "Requisites of a Lasting Peace" by Rhodes Scholar and Emory University professor Dr. William B. Stubbs; and a celebration of Twelfth Night according to old English custom. Children, grandchildren, and members of the Atlanta Woman's Club were invited. Activities included carol singing, zodiac readings, telling the story of the Twelfth Night and its significance, cake cutting, star hunting, a crowning of the king and queen, and refreshments. A special feature of the party was the cutting and

255 "Woman's Club Debs Entertain Lawson Soldiers," unidentified newspaper clipping, 21 December 1944, 1975–0487M, Georgia Federation of Women's Clubs, Fifth District Records, unit 19, Georgia Archives.

256 "Celebrating 100 Years of Excellence," *Tallulah Falls Magazine* 30/3 (Fall 2008): 27.

Past Atlanta Woman's Club presidents. From left to right: Mrs. Howard Pattillo, Mrs. B. M. Boykin, Mrs. Wm. P. Dunn, Mrs. John F. MacDougald (President), Mrs. Alonzo Richardson, Mrs. Alva G. Maxwell, Mrs. Claude C. Smith at AWC's 50th Birthday, Nov. 12, 1945

257 "Woman's Club to Present Three-Act Comedy on Jan. 19," *Atlanta Constitution*, 8 Jan 1945, 1975–0487M, Georgia Federation of Women's Clubs, Fifth District Records, unit 19, Georgia Archives; "Club Will Hear Judge Black," *Atlanta Constitution*, 5 Feb 1945, 1975–0487M; "Twelfth Night To Be Celebrated," *Atlanta Constitution*, 10 Jan 1945, 1975–0487M; "Tech Glee Club to Present Opera *Martha* May 2–3," *Georgia Press*, 7 Apr 1945, 1975–0487M; "Woman's Club to Meet, Hear Dr. Stubbs on 'Peace,'" *The Georgia Press—The Northside Press*, 10 February 1945, Georgia Archives acc. 1975–0487M, Georgia Federation of Women's Clubs, Fifth District Records, unit 19.

258 Houde, *Reaching Out*, 256–58.

259 Anderson, ed., "A Walk through History"; "Atlanta Woman's Club History #1," Wimbish House Archives.

pasting of Christmas card pictures in scrapbooks for children in sick wards of local hospitals.[257]

During this time, the women of the GFWC continued to emphasize the principles of nonpartisanship and the acceptance of club members as individuals. In culmination of their efforts, in 1945, when the war ended, representatives from the General Federation were invited to participate in a conference leading to the organization and establishment of the United Nations.[258]

In their transition from war to peace, members of the Atlanta Woman's Club joined other GFWC members in continuing their focus on a commitment to veterans, youth and their communities; raising world consciousness; international issues; and establishing closer ties with sister clubwomen of the US and other countries. By this time, media and communications had expanded to include both radio and television, consumerism was rampant, and prosperity reigned.

During 1948–1950, the Junior Section of the Georgia Federation was formally organized with the position of Junior Director and the body of Junior Section. These efforts reflected club members' need to increase membership and ensure that younger participants would continue the organization's work. Politically, the Atlanta Woman's Club supported efforts by the state Federation to bring forth legislation for premarital examinations, compulsory secret ballot in all Georgia counties, and a juvenile court bill to set up twenty-three district juvenile courts throughout the state.[259]

It was a time of reminiscence and looking toward the future as the women concentrated on the approaching second half of the century and rejoiced in the

Mrs. Howard Pattillo
1940–1943

Mrs. B. C. Settle
1943–1944

Mrs. John F. MacDougald
1944–1946

fiftieth anniversary of the Georgia Federation. Federation Celebration activities took place in Atlanta's Biltmore Hotel.[260]

By 1946, the Library Commission had been abolished and its services given to the state Department of Education, but the Atlanta Woman's Club never wavered in its support. Emphasis remained on youth as Georgia women focused on programs such as preschool training for children, programs for teens, recreation, and junior citizenship. Other initiatives included conservation and the preservation of the state's forests. In order to gain support for their causes, the Club included a speaker's bureau committee that was prepared to address local groups. Radio interviews and announcements of activities were made during rural-urban broadcasts over WSB (a call sign meaning "Welcome South, Brother"). In an ongoing effort, the Club hosted presentations by outstanding Georgia writers.[261]

By 1949, Georgia had turned the corner in industrial production, and the state was rapidly changing. Despite continuing poverty and isolation in outlying rural areas, for the first time "Georgia was a predominately manufacturing state instead of an agricultural one."[262]

As the Atlanta Woman's Club transitioned from the turbulent decade of the forties into the whirlwind changes of the fifties, many outstanding events took place. Among these were appearances by well-known authors, political figures, and other notable celebrities. Programs included a diversity of topics, including "Nuremburg Trials in Germany," "The Far East," "Tax Revision," "Salad and Sandwich Making," and "Flower Arranging." In addition, members continued to participate in a wide variety of activities, including bridge luncheons, teas, and other endeavors. Some of the highlights included a request to Georgia governor Herman Talmadge resulting in the proclamation of a January Georgia Products week. With the assistance of commissioner of agriculture Tom Linder, members sponsored a Georgia Products Parade, followed by a Georgia Products banquet with exhibits displayed in the Club. Georgia Products Committee members cooperated with the Made-in-Georgia Exposition Committee at the Southeastern Fair and participated

260 Houde, *Reaching Out*, 259–67; Anderson, ed., "A Walk through History."

261 Ibid.; Atlanta Woman's Club Bulletin, 1939–1940, pp. 29–33, MSS 353, Kenan Research Center.

262 Anderson, ed., "A Walk through History"; Atlanta Woman's Club History #1.

263 Mrs. Clarke Donaldson, editor-in-chief, *Atlanta Woman's Club Yearbook 1948–1950: Biennial Report*, courtesy Daisy Luckey Aukerman Woman's Club Archives, personal collection.

264 Ibid.

in several radio programs. All of this was in addition to the Club's annual Georgia Products dinner held several months later.[263]

Steering the Club through this difficult time were several capable women including Mrs. Howard Pattillo (1940–1943), Mrs. B. C. Settle (1943–1944), Mrs. John F. MacDougald (1944–1946), Mrs. J. Low Zachry (1946–1947), Mrs. E. E. Bengston (1947–1948), and Mrs. Clarke Donaldson (1948–1950). As always, members continued to advocate for reforms in all areas of civic life, awarded scholarships to deserving Georgia students, and gave immeasurable support to Tallulah Falls School.[264]

Mrs. J. Low Zachry
1946-1947

Mrs. E. E. Bengston
1947-1948

Mrs. Clarke Donaldson
1948-1950

CHAPTER SIXTEEN

Etiquette implies a respect for yourself and for those around you.

Amy Vanderbilt
Atlanta Woman's Club program speaker, 1961

he women of the Atlanta Woman's Club entered the 1950s with optimism intermingled with fear. The decade was punctuated by conflicts spurred by the growth of Communism and the threat of atomic destruction. During these Cold War years, the country experienced a continuation of prosperity, economic turbulence, and uneasiness. The years were characterized by a baby boom, a rise in home ownership, the spread of television, the beginnings of suburban sprawl, the building of bomb shelters, and concerns about the Korean War.[265]

Meanwhile, Atlanta was undergoing a massive transition as it became an international city and a hub for Southern business activities. All of Georgia was undergoing change as manufacturing became more dominant. The clubwomen continued to highlight their support of Georgia-made and Georgia-grown products with a Georgia Products Dinner.[266] The Municipal Market, always featuring Georgia's homegrown produce, had evolved from its humble beginnings to the "largest retail center for farm products in the state." The enterprise boasted more than 250 employees.[267]

Several great accomplishments marked these years: the Club refurbished its headquarters, began and completed a $40,000 expansion, and

265 Houde, *Reaching Out: A Story of the General Federation of Women's Clubs* (Washington/Chicago: Mobium Press, 1989) 269–75.

266 Mrs. Clyde F. Anderson, ed., "A Walk through History—Georgia Federation of Women's Clubs 1896–1986," paper, Wimbish House Archives, Atlanta GA; Biennial Report, Atlanta Woman's Club, 1950–1953, p.6. MSS 353 Kenan Research Center, Atlanta History Center, Atlanta GA.

267 Ann Taylor Boutwell, "The Sweet Spot: Sweet Auburn Curb Market Is an Atlanta Institution," *Intown-Buckhead-North Community* , unidentified clipping, collection, Wimbish House Archives.

268 Atlanta Woman's Club Biennial Report—1966–1968, p.50, MSS 353, Kenan Research Center.

269 Atlanta Woman's Club Yearbook: 1950–1952, Biennial Report, p 6, MSS 353, Kenan Research Center; Atlanta Woman's Club Biennial Report: 1952–1954, p. 18, courtesy Daisy Luckey Aukerman Woman's Club Archives Collection.

270 Ibid.

271 Atlanta Woman's Club Biennial Report: 1952–1954.

272 "'Your Life' Drama Tells Club's Progress: Woman's Club to Celebrate Opening of Wesley Hall," *Atlanta Journal*, 15 Sep 1954, Scrapbook #17, 1955–56, MSS 353, Kenan Research Center.

273 Ibid.

274 Unidentified article, Scrapbook #17, 1955–56, MSS 353; "AWC Celebrating its 59th Birthday," *Atlanta Journal*, 4 Nov 1954, Scrapbook #17, 1955–56, MSS 353.

275 Anderson, ed., "A Walk through History"; "Federation Women Asked to Continue War on Crime," *Atlanta Constitution*, 26 Sep 1958, F 2, R 96, U 5, S 3 flat -1049 048-01-00,1 unit 27; unidentified article, Scrapbook #17, 1955–56 MSS 353 Griffin, Lee, "Woman to Woman," *Atlanta Constitution*, F 2, R 96, U 5, S 3 flat -1049 048-01-001, unit 27, Georgia Archives.

paid off both mortgages, an event members celebrated with a "Burning of the Mortgage" ceremony.[268] Events during these years included bridge parties, antique and flower shows, a tea for the cast of *I'd Climb the Highest Mountain*, and hosting the Georgia Federation (GaFWC). As always, public personalities made appearances. These included Madame Aung Sang, the Rangoon, Burma, minister of health; two social service directors of West Berlin, Germany; film actress Mary Pickford; consuls of England, Austria, Italy, Peru, and Mexico; United States Representative and Mrs. James C. Davis; and Governor Herman E. Talmadge. "For the first time in history, a tape recording was made by members of the Club and sent to the American Woman's Club of Brussels, Belgium, who replied in turn."[269]

The arts remained an integral part of club life with emphasis on all forms, including drama. The club presented *These Things Are*, a play depicting its history, and many musicians and soloists performed for members' entertainment. Exhibits included portraits, oils, watercolors, and ceramics.[270] Members also participated in a "Get Out the Vote" campaign and donated hundreds of copies of the *Declaration of Independence* and the *United States Constitution* to Atlanta schools.

Interesting new features of the Atlanta Woman's Club were the offering of "Charm Schools," a "Modeling Class," and a directed reading course through the University of Georgia. Lectures were held on all phases of horticulture, including landscaping. One reason club members experienced such unusual and outstanding programs was that each year the "Program Contest" awarded a silver trophy to the "department, division or committee doing the most outstanding work."[271]

The tradition of Georgia Products week continued, with manufacturers exhibiting products in the Club building and Herman Talmadge attending as one of the featured speakers. Bridge parties were serious fundraisers, sometimes involving hundreds of card players. Throughout the years, members shared their experiences on trips abroad.[272]

In 1954, the Atlanta Woman's Club celebrated its fifty-ninth birthday in conjunction with the Fulton County Centennial and the Club's opening of the Cora Bell Wesley Banquet Hall. The highlight was the presentation of *Your Life*, which told of the Club's progress and events through the years. At dinner, a member dressed in 1895 attire led the group in singing.[273]

The $40,000 addition to the clubhouse and the construction of new rooms expanded the Club's venues for serving the community. The changes were such that four separate events could take place simultaneously, and these changes were the first major improvements in more than thirty years. The following year, the Club celebrated its sixtieth birthday by hosting a musical program featuring opera star Rita Griffith, along with Robert Harrison and Donovan Schumaker of the Atlanta Symphony Orchestra. Special activities included the Harvest Fair and a Travel Fashion Tea.[274]

Atlanta Woman's Club members' growing empowerment brought with it increased understanding and knowledge of the power of individuals and members as a group. With that followed the awareness of civic political responsibility as a force for positive action and change. The Club continued to wage war on crime and to address problems related to juveniles, jails, and the court system.[275]

A related area in which the Atlanta Woman's Club joined the Georgia Federation in demanding reform was in the "subhuman treatment" of the state's prisoners. Club members throughout the state wanted the "development of programs for rehabilitation, including classification centers, the developing of prison industry, increased use of probation services, and job placement for those eligible for parole."[276] These types of issues continue to be a focus today as the Atlanta Woman's Club lends its support to the Georgia Justice Project and the Georgia Innocence Project.

The Atlanta Woman's Club also joined other clubs in promoting the use of seat belts and in addressing concerns related to literacy, the effect of violence and sex in the media, the continuing problems of Georgia's juvenile justice system, civic responsibility, stiff penalties for drug dealers, and the passage of a Fugitive Fathers Bill.[277] Too, the Club supported the General Federation's focus on youth and the community, aging, internationalism, and civil defense. One Atlanta project sponsored a Girl's Club.[278]

Atlanta Woman's Club members were particularly interested in help for the mentally, physically, and developmentally disabled. They conducted Easter egg hunts for the children at Cave Springs School for the Deaf; donated recordings and put on a square dance benefit for the blind; and furnished current magazines, clothing, and therapy materials for Grady Hospital.

As the years progressed, the women did not forget their commitment to support the arts and self-improvement, frequently combining interesting programs related to needlework, music, art, opera, writing, and lectures with opportunities for socializing and fun. They participated in diverse programs related to antiques, gardening, communications, and education. Activities included teas, fashion shows, bridge, gardening tours, flower shows, and tree plantings. Members participated in reading groups; provided scholarships to local students; hosted events for international students, visitors, and consulates; and attended legislative and political meetings. Three of the most exciting events for members were having the Atlanta Woman's Club president Mrs. W. Beverly Johnson represent the Club at the 1955 International Federation Convention in Geneva, Switzerland; conducting a novel-writing contest; and having Captain Douglas Cordiner as speaker. Captain Cordiner was one of seven men who were the first explorers to land a plane at the South Pole and plant the American flag.[279]

As always, the Atlanta Woman's Club and other members of the Georgia Federation focused on Tallulah Falls School. In the mid-fifties, a master plan was developed to modernize the facilities. These plans included a new president's house, an athletic field house, a modern classroom building, and a library.[280]

At this time Atlanta was experiencing rapid development and change in the downtown area, particularly along Peachtree Street. Many old homes and businesses were sold and replaced by modern office buildings. In 1954, the Georgia Historical Commissioner placed a historical marker in front of the Atlanta Woman's Club's Wimbish House. In February 1956, the clubwomen established the "Memory Lane" endowment fund from gifts in honor of deceased members, relatives, and friends. Members still contribute to this fund, which has grown steadily through the years. Due to a bequest from Cora Bell Wesley, the Club was able to fund the Cora Bell

276 "Women's Clubs Demand Georgia Prison Reforms," unidentified clipping, F 2, R 96, U 5, S 3 flat -1049 048-01-001 unit #27.

277 "Timeline 2010," Women's History and Resource Center, General Federation of Women's Clubs, Washington, DC; Anderson, ed., "A Walk through History."

278 Houde, *Reaching Out*, 269–75; Anderson, ed., "A Walk through History"; Atlanta Woman's Club Biennial Report—1966–1968, p. 50, MSS 353.

279 1956–1958 Yearbook; Atlanta Woman's Club Biennial Report—1966–1968, p.50. MSS 353, Kenan Research Center, Atlanta History Center; Club Activities, pp. 38–41, Wimbish House Archives.

280 "Celebrating 100 Years of Excellence"; Anderson, ed., "A Walk through History."

281 1956–1958 Yearbook; "Club Activities," collection, Wimbish House Archives.

282 1956–1958 Yearbook.

283 Anderson, ed., "A Walk through History."

284 Atlanta Woman's Club: Biennial Report: 1956–1958, courtesy Daisy Luckey Aukerman Woman's Club Archives Collection.

285 Atlanta Woman's Club Yearbook: 1958–1960, courtesy Daisy Luckey Aukerman Woman's Club Archives Collection; Georgiana, 1 May 1959, vol. 20, no. 4, Official Publication of the GF of Business and Professional Women's Clubs Inc., file box 2, AC 1975–0487m, p. 2, Georgia Archives.

Wesley Hall, deemed one of the decade's greatest clubhouse improvements.[281]

The ladies of the Atlanta Woman's Club worked with a large number of community organizations including the Girls Club, Campfire Girls, and Girl Scouts and "cooperated in every community program."[282] As members of the Georgia Federation, the Atlanta Woman's Club helped in the purchase of a cannery for Tallulah Falls School. During the summer of 1956, as a fundraising event for the school, the Georgia Federation and Young Matrons Circle for Tallulah Falls School co-sponsored the premier of Walt Disney's movie *The Great Locomotive Chase.*[283]

Throughout these years, Atlanta Woman's Club members extended their ideas of the preservation and the values of their heritage to a heightened interest in antiques. The Antiques Study group offered programs related to almost everything old, from antique silver to dolls. The Club also participated as usual in the Harvest Fair. Among the Club's booth attractions was an appearance by Mrs. S. R. Dull, who autographed copies of her famous cookbook, *Southern Cooking.*[284]

In 1958 and 1959, in addition to their regular activities, members participated in giving book reviews on the Dean Dickens' *Party Line* television show, presented a dramatic interpretation of Somerset Maugham's *Rain,* gave a fall fashion show, participated on a panel at Georgia Tech for the Fabric Maintenance Conference, and continued to support and work with foreign students. Among the Atlanta Woman's Club's other projects was collaborating with Rich's department store in presenting community events. To cite one example, Rich's Business Woman's Board presented an event called "Fun, Food, Fashion" in which the club members participated.[285]

On a more serious level, the Atlanta Woman's Club, as a member of the Georgia Federation, joined other member clubs in promoting the first Governor's Conference on Education and advocated for getting children out of Georgia's prisons. "In 1957, the president of the Georgia Federation appointed a special Youth Service Committee to work toward getting the children out of jail." The committee's work resulted in the organizing of the Georgia Committee of the National Council on Crime and Delinquency.[286]

Mrs. Robert A. Long
1950–1951

Mrs. Olin S. Cofer
1951–1952

Mrs. James N. Brawner, Sr.
1952–1954

Mrs. W. Beverly Johnson
1954–1956

Mrs. J. Wen Lundeen
1956–1958

Mrs. John P. Coleman
1958–1960

Still expanding, the GFWC purchased a building adjacent to its headquarters to use as an annex. On the national level, the organization influenced local clubs and federations to support citizen participation; voting campaigns; the promotion of American values, including God and country and the American Heritage; preservation of democracy; patriotism; and efforts to promote mental health, as well as their ongoing programs on education and the arts. In keeping with the General Federation's emphasis on our nation's heritage, members of the GaFWC joined in contributing monies toward the restoration of Philadelphia's Independence Hall.[287]

Atlanta Woman's Club presidents during the fifties included Mrs. Robert A. Long (1950–1951), Mrs. Olin S. Cofer (1951–1952), Mrs. James N. Brawner Sr. (1952–1954), Mrs. W. Beverly Johnson (1954–1956), Mrs. J. Wen Lundeen (1956–1958), and Mrs. John P. Coleman (1958–1960).[288]

[286] Anderson, ed., "A Walk through History."

[287] Houde, *Reaching Out*, 277–309; Anderson, ed., "A Walk through History."

[288] "Presidents' List," Wimbish House Archives.

CHAPTER SEVENTEEN

Joining with other great national voluntary organizations of our country, the General Federation has given a new meaning to citizen volunteer participation in programs with and for hospitalized veterans. American clubwomen, making ever-increasing and significant contributions to our medical care and treatment programs, are an integral and essential part of the Veterans Administration's hospital team.

Joseph H. McNinch[289]
Former Chief Medical Director, Veterans Administration

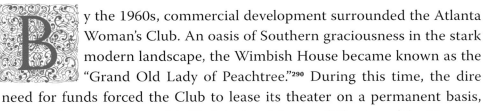y the 1960s, commercial development surrounded the Atlanta Woman's Club. An oasis of Southern graciousness in the stark modern landscape, the Wimbish House became known as the "Grand Old Lady of Peachtree."[290] During this time, the dire need for funds forced the Club to lease its theater on a permanent basis, entering into a contract with Christopher Manos of Theater of the Stars, an arrangement that lasted into the early eighties.

Formerly called the Community Playhouse, the facility underwent a major renovation taking the new name Peachtree Playhouse. Described by Manos as perhaps one of the best venues for seeing plays in the Southeast, the theater had improvements that included an addition to the lobby and a gallery of photos recalling plays of Theater of the Stars' prior years in Atlanta, which provided a glimpse into Atlanta theatrical history. The

289 Houde, *Reaching Out: A Story of the General Federation of Women's Clubs* (Washington/Chicago: Mobium Press, 1989) 331.

290 Scott, Jeffrey, "Historic Atlanta: Woman's Club Plans to Reopen After Fire," unidentified clipping, Wimbish House Archives.

291 "Peachtree Playhouse: Renovated Theater Gives Impression of Broadway House," unidentified article, Atlanta Woman's Club Papers *1, Wimbish House Archives.

292 Insertion within Atlanta Woman's Club Scrapbook 24/26, 1960–1962/ 1964–1966, 76–214–26, MSS 353, Kenan Research Center, Atlanta History Center.

293 Margaret Turner, "Get Your Manners Tuned for Courtesy," *Atlanta Journal-Constitution* clipping, Atlanta Woman's Club Scrapbook 24, 1960– 1962, 76–214–26, MSS 353, Kenan Research Center, Atlanta History Center.

294 Mrs. Clyde F. Anderson, ed., "A Walk through History—Georgia Federation of Women's Clubs 1896– 1986," paper, Wimbish House Archives, Atlanta GA; "Celebrating 100 Years of Excellence," *Tallulah Falls School Magazine* 30/3 (Fall 2008): 29, in Wimbish House Archives.

295 Houde, *Reaching Out*, 323.

296 Anderson, ed., "A Walk through History."

297 "Timeline 2010," Women's History and Resource Center, General Federation of Women's Clubs, Washington DC; Houde, *Reaching Out*, 313–57.

winter play season opened with *Summer and Smoke*, a Tennessee Williams play costarring Eva Marie Saint and Ronny Cox.[291]

The Atlanta Woman's Club entered the uneasiness of the decade's early years with concerns about the country's political stability in the wake of assassinations, racial and urban unrest, the space race, and the Vietnam War. Members reflected the General Federation's efforts in their support and concern for veterans, their help for those in need overseas, and their emphasis on international relations, including work for organizations such as CARE and UNICEF. Distress at the plight of the nation's Native Americans and the preservation of Native American culture also remained a national and local issue. In fall 1960, the Atlanta Woman's Club held a program on "Indian Affairs" with Forest J. Gerard, tribal relations officer for the US Public Health Service, as guest speaker. The event included a demonstration of Native American dances by the order of the Arrow Dance Team, whose members dressed in authentic costumes.[292]

That same year, governor Ernest Vandiver proclaimed 23–29 October "Courtesy Week in Georgia." Joining in the festivities, the Atlanta Woman's Club held a "Brunch for Courtesy" sponsored jointly with the Atlanta Chapter of American Business Clubs. The highlight was a program by etiquette expert Amy Vanderbilt, author of the bestselling "Complete Book of Etiquette."[293]

In celebration of the Golden Anniversary of Tallulah Falls School, October 1960 was declared "Tallulah Falls School Month in Georgia" by proclamation of Governor Ernest Vandiver, who paid special tribute to the school for the service it rendered to education in the state. By 1962, the school was rated as one of the top twenty-five small high schools in the United States, and, in 1963, two new dormitories opened: Westmoreland Hall for girls and Ida Fitzpatrick Hall for boys.[294]

Locally, changes resulting from urbanization and population growth presented the Atlanta Woman's Club and other General Federation clubs with numerous challenges. The spread of suburbia altered lifestyles as the women found themselves in a "fast, new, accelerated world." Concerns grew over this new era's environmental impact.[295]

Aware of some Georgia residents' lack of access to higher education, GaFWC clubwomen were instrumental in helping to pass a bill establishing junior colleges in several areas of the state. They also pressed for measures to improve literacy rates.[296]

Emphasizing their nonpartisanship, the Atlanta Woman's Club and other GFWC members continued to encourage knowledge and participation in civic and international relations, the development of leadership skills, mental and physical health and welfare, conservation and beautification projects, auto safety, personal commitment, help for veterans, juvenile justice, and individual responsibility. They also addressed issues related to urban problems, a decline in membership, and the growing need for expanded international outreach.[297]

Members of the International Affairs Department of the Atlanta Woman's Club conducted study programs related to the Alliance for Progress, the Peace Corps, the United Nations, the Common Market, Arms Control, and NATO. They also corresponded with other clubwomen around the world and distributed copies of the "Universal Declaration of Human Rights." They were so enthusiastic in these endeavors that the Georgia Federation (GaFWC) Convention named them first-place winners in International Affairs and presented them with a beautiful silver five-branch candelabra.

Due to growing concerns related to the Cold War, club members were reminded to keep food, water, and first aid supplies on hand in their homes in case of a nuclear attack. The women participated in a variety of community drives, worked at polls during elections, helped in a booth for Mental Health at the Southeastern Fair, and continued to lend tremendous support to veterans. In 1963, the Atlanta Woman's Club was represented in the Armistice Day Parade by the use of a car sponsored by the American Legion of Atlanta. Never did the Club fail to support its community's arts: members awarded scholarships; sponsored performances, exhibits, and readings; and dedicated themselves to the "promotion of fine poetry."[298]

A special fundraising project for Tallulah Falls School included an organ recital in the Atlanta Woman's Club auditorium. "The Alverson Piano Company of Decatur, Georgia, furnished the organ and the artist. The Club had a booth at the State Fair grounds with a sign advertising Tallulah Falls School and the recital. Members of the Atlanta Woman's Club distributed literature and sold tickets." Photographs of the school were displayed at the Merchandise Mart, where members also provided information and tickets. The event was publicized over radio and television and in local newspapers.

In 1964, Atlanta Woman's Club member Mrs. J. S. Roberts traveled to Detroit to receive a Concert Artists Guild award given to the Atlanta Symphony Orchestra for work with talented young artists. She remarked, "Credit goes to the Music Division of the Atlanta Woman's Club, working with audition winners and sponsoring them to perform before other civic groups, for this award."[299] Other projects of the AWC included their continuing support of Georgia products and local merchants, Arbor Day, and foreign exchange students. One of the Club's most successful enterprises of this time was the Georgia Arts and Industry Exhibit at the Harvest Fair.[300]

The Atlanta Woman's Club's unrelenting devotion to local, state, national, and international causes resulted in numerous Fifth District, national, and state awards and citations. One such project was an unusual Community Improvement program during which members made an outdoor mini-park on the roof of a nurse's dormitory at Grady Hospital. By the end of the project, the site's barren, graveled surface had been "turned into a lovely place with picnic tables, benches, lounging chairs, hanging baskets of flowers and a slatted wooden floor." Club president Mrs. Edward O. (Kathryn) Snow "held an open house on the roof for the students, faculty and clubwomen when the project was finished," and "before and after pictures of the area were on the front cover of the National Awards publication of the Community Improvement Program at the General Federation Convention." The club was also commended by Meals for Millions, CARE, and Radio Free Europe.[301]

In 1965, Atlanta Club members joined in the celebration of the seventy-fifth anniversary of the General Federation of Women's Clubs. By that time, Junior Clubs had become more active and Juniorette Clubs were being formed for girls between ages fourteen and eighteen. As women from young to old joined in the festivities, the

298 *Atlanta Woman's Club Yearbook: 1962–1964*, courtesy Daisy Luckey Aukerman Woman's Club Archives, personal collection.

299 Ibid.

300 Atlanta Woman's Club Scrapbook 25, 1960–1962, 76–214–25, MSS 353, Kenan Research Center, Atlanta History Center; *Atlanta Woman's Club Yearbook: 1962–1964*. Courtesy of Daisy Luckey Aukerman AWC Archives Personal Collection.

301 Atlanta Woman's Club Biennial Report—1966–1968, p. 51, MSS 353, Kenan Research Center, Atlanta History Center.

Paintings by Emily Grigsby in the Wimbish House. The painting on the left is hanging in the sunroom, formerly known as the Palm Room. The painting on the right is hanging in a top-floor bedroom. *Photographer: Aryc W. Mosher*

302 "Timeline 2010;" Houde, *Reaching Out*, 339.

303 Atlanta Woman's Club Biennial Report—1966–1968, p. 51, MSS 353, Kenan Research Center, Atlanta History Center..

304 *Atlanta Woman's Club Year Book, 1968–1970*, p. 15, courtesy Daisy Luckey Aukerman Woman's Club Archives, personal collection.

United States Post Office awarded the General Federation a stamp in honor of the occasion carrying the name of the General Federation of Women's Clubs and depicting two women attired in styles that spanned the years of GFWC history.[302]

Locally, the Atlanta Woman's Club was honored by the naming of a 1966 *Hemerocallis* (daylily) in celebration of the Club's seventieth anniversary. Named the "Diamond Celebration," the plant commemorates the Atlanta Woman's Club wherever it is planted.[303]

Among the interesting experiences Atlanta Woman's Club members shared during these years were a "Tasting Party" with German gourmet specialties prepared by two German chefs and sponsored by the Federation of German Agricultural Export Industries and Lufthansa German Airlines; a Hawaiian Luau; and promotional appearances by Georgia authors as well as other inspirational writers.[304]

Addressing members' attempts to gain knowledge and self-improvement, the Club continued to sponsor many lectures and studies on currents issues and events. Programs included "Crime and Delinquency," "Air and Water Pollution," "Prevention of Mental Illness and Promotion of Mental Health," "Art of Living and Understanding Art," "Inspirational Writing," "Opening Doors to International Understanding," "Cambodia," and other timely topics.

As was custom, club members gave enormous support for Atlanta's arts. For example, the Music Division of the Atlanta Woman's Club promoted musical enrichment throughout the Club and community. Programs brought in talented musicians and emphasized "all types of music to include opera, strings, woodwind instruments, piano, vocal soloists, and a very informative lecture and demonstration on ballet dancing."[305]

Members expanded their studies to embrace hymns representing different faiths, including "those of the earlier centuries, keeping in mind that a great hymn must have music of the highest conception and also a worthy text."[306] Members of the Music Division also personally fashioned crafts and handmade articles and sewed items for the annual Symphony Boutique. They provided music scholarships and volunteered time as office assistants who were responsible for monthly mailings and telephone campaigns to promote ticket sales for concerts and the performing arts. The Music Division's devotion earned them special recognition by the National Federation of Music Clubs. A student attending Julliard sent a letter thanking the Atlanta Woman's Club and its Music Division for the opportunity he had received in furthering his musical education.

Many members of the Club were accomplished musicians. For instance, Mrs. Ruth McDonald, the 1969 program chairman of the Music Division, was "an accomplished pianist, a graduate of the Julliard School of Music, and on the faculty of Georgia State University."[307] Elegant and talented Woman's Club member Emily Bourne Grigsby, described as "a role model for woman's achievement," was a model, artist, professional mediator, arbitrator, attorney, writer, and opera singer. In the latter capacity, she helped form the Opera Arts, one of the first Atlanta opera companies, and she served as president of the Atlanta Music Club. Both organizations held events in the Club auditorium. Later, in the 1990s, Mrs. Grigsby would generously donate several of her paintings to help refurbish the Wimbish House following a devastating fire.[308]

These years were met with increasing concern about crime. Atlanta Woman's Club president Mrs. Edward O. Snow appointed a citizens committee to meet with members of the Crime Committee, the chief of police, and other city officials to determine how to tackle Atlanta's crime and narcotics crisis. Members were heavily involved in learning about and addressing issues of crime prevention and juvenile justice; they even attended juvenile court and hosted juvenile court judge John S. Langford as a guest speaker. These issues became paramount in the early seventies as a "hippie" community surrounded the Woman's Club complex.[309]

Future clubwomen traced a marked decline in membership to crime rates during the sixties. According to Atlanta Woman's Club president Mrs. Curtis H. (Mildred) Bryant (1982–1984), the public was afraid to come into the area because there were so many muggings. In fact, clubs all over the country were beginning to lose members. Times were changing and women were increasingly entering the work force due to economic need and the desire to explore new opportunities.[310]

Women also looked to professional organizations to provide venues for business networking. Still, the Atlanta Woman's Club presented to the community an enthusiastic, hardworking membership, continuing to reach out in areas of need as well as in its support of ongoing programs such as the prevention of drug abuse, forest conservation, and Tallulah Falls School.

305 *Atlanta Woman's Club Year Book, 1968–1970*, p. 26, courtesy Daisy Luckey Aukerman Woman's Club Archives, personal collection.

306 Ibid., 27.

307 Ibid., 28.

308 Interview by Anne B. Jones with Emily Bourne Grigsby, November 2010.

309 Atlanta Woman's Club Yearbook 1968–1970, p. 32, MSS 353; Ada Biehl, "Woman's Club Celebrates 75th Year Serving City," *Atlanta Journal-Constitution*, 1 Nov 1970, Wimbish House Archives.

310 Martha Woodham, "Time Takes Toll On Woman's Club," *The Atlanta Constitution*, 1 Apr 1985, Wimbish House Archives; Atlanta Woman's Club #1, Wimbish House Archives.

311 Milo Ippolito, "Curb Market Milestone," *Atlanta-Journal Constitution*, 9 Oct 2003, Wimbish House Archives.

312 "President's List," Wimbish House Archives.

During this period, the Atlanta Municipal Market was also entering a period of decline. Interstate construction sliced through its neighborhood as suburbs arose, and the tension of integration caused many customers to avoid African-American shopping areas. It would be years before the market would regain its prominence.[311]

Presidents during this period were Mrs. Frank L. Picotte (1960–1962), Mrs. W. Grady Bowen (1962–1963), Mrs. Joe L. Hewell Sr. (1963–1966), Mrs. W. A. Armistead (1966–1968), and Mrs. Edward O. Snow (1968–1972).[312]

Mrs. Frank L. Picotte
1960-1962

Mrs. W. Grady Bowen
1962-1963

Mrs. Joe L. Hewell, Sr.
1963-1966

Mrs. W. A. Armistead
1966-1968

Mrs. Edward O. Snow
1968-1972

CHAPTER EIGHTEEN

The traditional women's organizations that for decades have championed women's rights to vote, to work, to be educated and to serve their communities are facing a challenge from a liberation movement that many consider bizarre, alien and totally unacceptable.

Lacey Fosburgh, 1970[313]

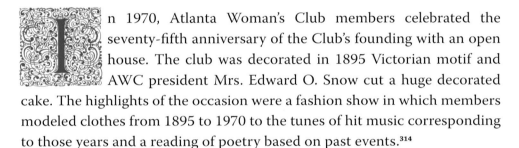In 1970, Atlanta Woman's Club members celebrated the seventy-fifth anniversary of the Club's founding with an open house. The club was decorated in 1895 Victorian motif and AWC president Mrs. Edward O. Snow cut a huge decorated cake. The highlights of the occasion were a fashion show in which members modeled clothes from 1895 to 1970 to the tunes of hit music corresponding to those years and a reading of poetry based on past events.[314]

The early 1970s were challenging for the Atlanta Woman's Club as members faced issues related to political discontent and cultural change. Longtime conservative advocates of women's rights, they found themselves facing an age when radical activist groups took center stage and demanded swift change. The question for club members was what attitude to take. Should they lend support to this new breed of women or hold back, play it safe, and try to exert change through traditional means?

The more vocal and demonstrative champions of the women's liberation movement were effecting change throughout the nation, not only on the political scene, but also among women themselves. Many in the AWC, Georgia Federation, and General Federation continued to seek refuge in the

---

313 Lacey Fosburgh, "Clubs Caught With Head in Sand," *Atlanta Constitution*, 9 Sep 1970, vol. 30, Georgia Federation of Women's Clubs Fifth District Records, 1896–1972, accn. 1975–0487M, manuscripts section, Georgia Department of Archives and History, Atlanta GA.

314 Ada Biehl, "Woman's Club Celebrates 75th Year Serving City," *Atlanta Journal-Constitution*, 1 Nov 1970, Wimbish House Archives, Atlanta GA; President's Report by Mrs. Edward O. Snow, 1970–1972, Wimbish House Archives.

315 Fosburgh, "Clubs Caught With Head in Sand"; President's Report by Snow, 1970–1972.

316 President's Report by Snow, 1970–1972.

317 Floyd, Mary, "Angela's Election Not a Surprise, Inauguration Was," *Savannah Evening Press*, 30 Apr 1970, vol. 30, Georgia Federation of Women's Clubs, Fifth District Records, 1896–1972, AC 1975–0487M.

318 *Atlanta Woman's Club Year Book 1970–1972*, p. 14, courtesy Daisy Luckey Aukerman Woman's Club Archives Collection; "Man Needs Discipline: Pollution is a Personal Problem." *Atlanta Journal and Constitution*, vol. 30, Fifth District Records, 1896–1972, 1975–0487M; Georgia Federation of Women's Clubs, 1896–1971, pp. 21–22, *Atlanta Journal and Constitution*, vol. 30, Fifth District Records, 1896–1972, AC 1975–0487M; *Georgia Clubwoman 1971* 30/88, p. 16, Fifth District Records, 1896–1972, AC 1975–0487M; President's Report by Snow, 1970–1972.

319 *Atlanta Woman's Club Yearbook 1970–1972*, pp. 35–36.

320 Unidentified clipping from *Atlanta Journal and Constitution*, vol. 30, Fifth District Records, 1896–1972, AC 1975–0487M; *Atlanta Woman's Club Yearbook 1970–1972*.

old ways. They did not know what to make of the sometimes militant women whose behavior defied decades of feminine protocol. The harder the women of the new movement pushed, the more entrenched the others became. Throughout the country women reacted, sometimes with skepticism, hostility, indifference, or ignorance and frequently in fear.[315]

Most of the women of the Atlanta Woman's Club and other sister clubs were likely to contact their political representatives, usually by mail, to request support for legislation related to women's rights as well as other issues dear to their hearts. The methods of the liberationists threatened their view of women's roles in their families and their communities. They were afraid of political backlash and the ultimate price they might pay for sweeping reform.

At the time, the General Federation of Women's Clubs had 11 million members. "We're conservative and constructive," stated the organization's executive secretary Mrs. Wilson Christian, who echoed the sentiments of many of the women. As a whole, the clubwomen believed that change should come about through time and education and that women should cling to feminine traditions.[316]

Despite the debate, Georgia women began to present themselves in more modern roles. In 1970, symbolizing women's sense of power, the Georgia Federation's new Junior Conference president and third vice president, Angela (Mrs. Ashley K.) Dearing, and the new Georgia Federation president, Jerry Peters, each showed up at the GaFWC's formal installation banquet wearing a pantsuit. Mrs. Dearing's pantsuit was accented with flowing pink chiffon. Mrs. Peter's was constructed of flowing black lace.[317]

Less volatile issues the women continued to address included urbanization, energy conservation, crime and its prevention, drug abuse, pollution, dwindling membership, and an increasingly fast-paced environment. They continued to focus on programs related to self-improvement, good government, patriotism, preservation, international relations, and service. Bonded through mutual determination and good will, they continued to emphasize sisterhood. In 1970 and 1972, Atlanta Woman's Club president Mrs. Edward O. Snow summed up members' feelings when she stated, "As we go through life we realize that Memory is a Rosary that constitutes perhaps our greatest wealth. This wealth is not so much in deeds well done, as it is in the splendid enriching friendships we form from day to day in organizations such as ours."[318]

During Mrs. Snow's administration, members enjoyed exploring such topics as "Creative Writing," "History of Music in the South," "The Hero in Modern Literature," and "Writing of Poetry." Study topics included "Present Day Germany," "Scotland," "Laos," "India Today," "What About China?," "The Atlanta Foreign Policy Conference," and, in particular, issues related to the withdrawal from Vietnam.[319]

The women continued to support area events such as the Harvest Fair and to keep themselves well informed on issues related to art, history, and other academic subjects. Among their popular guests was director of the Atlanta Historical Society, Franklin Garrett.[320]

Their concerns and interests reflected those of the General Federation. In 1975, the GFWC received a major grant from the US Department of Justice Law

Enforcement Assistance Administration to activate "Hands Up," a national program designed to promote awareness of the citizen's role in preventing and combating crime. The following year, the GFWC established a Trust Fund for the Arts in partnership with Affiliate Artists, Inc., to support nationwide young artist-in-residence programs. In 1977, GFWC clubwomen participated in International Women's Year programs, meetings on women's issues, and the National Conference for Women. In 1978, in partnership with Owens-Corning, GFWC developed a nationwide "Home Energy Check" program to encourage energy conservation.[321]

Crime had a direct impact on Atlanta Woman's Club members. Many continued to believe the Club's downtown location was dangerous. The women longed for new, more youthful participants but membership continued to decline, not only because more women had entered the workforce and could not attend daytime meetings, but also because the Club's location provoked fear. The club women made concentrated efforts to help the area's young people by working with youth centers.[322]

During the mid-seventies, Atlanta Woman's Club members worked on projects related to the United States' Bicentennial and the International Affairs Department of the Georgia Federation to institute a model United Nations Security Council. The effort involved high school students from throughout Georgia. Students' expenses were paid and chaperones were provided for the three-day event at Tallulah Falls School, where "participants gleaned a better understanding of our position in world affairs and the necessity for world cooperation in achieving world peace."[323]

Georgia Federation members also established a fund to build a chapel at Tallulah Falls School. To raise money for the project and to help save Atlanta's Fox Theater from destruction, they cooperated with the school's Young Matrons Circle in sponsoring a play called "Happening at the Fabulous Fox." The benefit featured Harry Belafonte and his Las Vegas Revue.

Legislative issues continued to be a focus of the Club and of the GaFWC as the women sought to promote progress in areas such as juvenile justice, child abuse, and rape laws. The Atlanta Woman's Club, then as now, lent support to the Ronald McDonald House, often called "The House that Love Built." The facility is "a place for parents and their children needing care at a nearby hospital" and serves as "a home away from home." Members of the Georgia Federation of Women's Clubs were so generous with their money, time, and donations that they were honored at the home's dedication by McDonald's founder Ray Kroc, who praised the organization's work in making the house a dream come true. As always, the AWC joined in supporting statewide, national, and global projects.[324]

The decade of the 1970s brought major changes and events for Tallulah Falls School. In 1970, the Young Matrons Circle Building was completed, TFS became privately chartered, and the school was named one of ten outstanding schools in Georgia. In 1972, TFS accepted its first exchange students, who traveled from Brazil. In 1975, Carol Stevens Hancock published *The Light in the Mountains*, which chronicled the school's history. Later in 1979, the Atlanta Woman's Club dedicated the Norwood Key Taylor Chapel.[325]

321 "Timeline 2010," Women's History and Resource Center, General Federation of Women's Clubs, Washington DC.

322 Woodham, Martha, "Time Takes Toll on Woman's Club," 1 Apr 1985, unidentified clipping, collection, Wimbish House Archives; *Atlanta Woman's Club Year Book 1970–1972*, p. 40.

323 Mrs. Clyde F. Anderson, ed., "A Walk through History—Georgia Federation of Women's Clubs 1896–1986," paper, Wimbish House Archives, Atlanta GA.

324 Ibid.

325 "Celebrating 100 Years of Excellence," *Tallulah Falls School Magazine* 30/3 (Fall 2008): 30–31, Wimbish House Archives.

326 Unidentified clipping, *Intown-Buckhead-North Community*, collection, Wimbish House Archives; letter from Greg Schneider, Survey and National Register Specialist, to Mrs. Lucy Willard, 2 Mar 1995, Wimbish House Archives.

327 From undated letters and notes included in Wimbish House Archives.

In 1976, the Sweet Auburn Curb Market (Municipal Market) and Sweet Auburn Historic District were placed on the National Register of Historic Places. In 1979, the Atlanta Woman's Club's treasured Wimbish House headquarters was officially added to the register, in addition to its listing on the Georgia Register of Historic Places.[326] This was an important step in recognizing the property's historical and architectural importance and demonstrating the need to preserve it.

Presidents during the decade of the 1970s were Mrs. Leroy H. Fargason (1972–1974), Mrs. H. Ragland Neathery (1974–1976), Mrs. Leroy H. Fargason (1976–1978), and Mrs. M. M. Harris, Sr. (1978–1980).[327]

Mrs. LeRoy H. Fargason
1972–1974 & 1976–1978

Mrs. H. Ragland Neathery
1974–1976

Mrs. M. M. Harris, Sr.
1978–1980

CHAPTER NINETEEN

A well informed citizenry is the keystone of our democratic society. The General Federation of Women's Clubs has made a major contribution toward this goal through promotion of full and free discussion of public issues.

Maurine B. Newberger[328]

By the 1980s, the Atlanta Woman's Club membership had dropped to just over 200 members, most of whom were middle-aged or older. Club presidents tried to attract new members while struggling to keep the Club financially sound despite the drain of constant maintenance. As one source of revenue, the Club's leasing of the auditorium, by then called the Peachtree Playhouse, to the Theater of the Stars attracted many of the city's theater patrons and featured such notable actors as Joe. E. Brown, E. G. Marshall, Jeanne Crain, and Loretta Swit. Another revenue-producing endeavor was the hosting of receptions. Members were able to obtain rent by leasing the second floor to elderly single women, who also provided clubhouse security. Under president Mrs. Curtis H. (Mildred) Bryant (1982–1984), the clubhouse began a complete renovation including the installation of smoke alarms.[329]

The elegant revived beauty of the Wimbish House and its facilities led to a revival in membership. During the 1984 convention of the GaFWC, the Atlanta Woman's Club was presented an award for the largest increase in membership among state clubs.[330]

328 Communication from Maurine B. Newberger, United States senator from Oregon, to the General Federation of Women's Clubs Headquarters, 1962–1964, in Houde, *Reaching Out: A Story of the General Federation of Women's Clubs* (Washington/Chicago: Mobium Press, 1989) 326–28.

329 Martha Woodham, "Time Takes Toll on Woman's Club," *Atlanta* Constitution, 1 Apr 1985, Wimbish House Archives, Atlanta GA; Margaret Reynolds, "Woman's Club Presented Portrait of Mrs. Bryant," unidentified clipping, Wimbish House Archives; Mrs. Curtis H. Bryant, "President's Report 1982–83," Wimbish House Archives; Bailey, Sharon, "Grand Old Lady Showing Her Age," *The Atlanta Constitution*, Monday, 6 Apr 1981, Wimbish House Archives.

330 Reynolds, Margaret, "Grand Old Lady Restored," *The Atlanta Northstar*, 12 July 1984, collection, Wimbish House Archives.

331 "Celebrating 100 Years of Excellence," *Tallulah Falls School Magazine* 30/3 (Fall 2008): 30–31, Wimbish House Archives.

332 Mrs. Clyde F. Anderson, ed., "A Walk through History—Georgia Federation of Women's Clubs 1896–1986," paper, Wimbish House Archives, Atlanta GA.

333 Bryant, "President's Report 1982–83," paper, Wimbish House Archives.

334 Ibid.

Atlanta Woman's Club members' support of Tallulah Falls School was unfaltering. The women celebrated the institution's seventy-fifth anniversary and helped prepare the students and the school for the world of computers. As if to signal this technological leap, students submitted the winning entry in the contest to name the new United States space shuttle. Their entry, "Endeavour," was selected from among 6,000 entries nationwide.[331]

Drawing on the school's "Light in the Mountains" heritage, the anniversary theme was "Continuing to Tend the Light." To mark the occasion, clubs of the Georgia Federation established a 75th Anniversary Perpetual Scholarship Fund, contributed money and books to expand the library, and increased other scholarship fund opportunities.

With the increasing role of women's participation in governmental affairs, women of the Atlanta Woman's Club and other organizations found themselves taking a more active and open role in Georgia politics. During the early eighties, the Club joined the state federation in lobbying the Georgia General Assembly for the passage of Georgia's first child restraint law; legislation providing juvenile court justices with child social case information; stricter and fairer DUI laws; a law prohibiting excessively dark tinting of vehicle windows; and legislation that eliminated sales tax on prescription drugs, eyeglasses, and contact lenses. Clubwomen were instrumental in preventing the passage of a bill that would remove the requirement that motorcyclists wear helmets. Members also participated in efforts to increase public awareness of energy conservation, literacy, toxic waste hazards, special needs children, and healthcare issues. One of their major 1985 projects was lobbying the state to install safety crossing arms on all school buses.[332]

The Atlanta Woman's Club continued its traditional programs, events, and activities and held lovely entertaining luncheons and teas. Bridge parties were among the most popular events, and the Club added new bridge tables. Rental fees for weddings and other special occasions held in the clubhouse and on the grounds helped fund the never-ending upkeep such a large complex required.[333]

In the early eighties, the Club refurbished the ballroom to make it more appealing as an event venue, and its freshly painted walls and refinished floors gave the Club's rental business a much-needed boost. Until the mid-eighties, the Club continued to rent the two upstairs bedrooms to single women, which generated additional income as well as the security of having full-time residents.

In 1989, the Club leased the space that once housed the Peachtree Playhouse Theatre to the Landsdown Corporation under a twenty-year contract. After a major renovation designed to "restore the building to its former glory" the corporation converted it into a popular entertainment complex featuring a café, dance club, tent-covered outdoor event area, and English gardens. Although it has changed names and management several times, the space has been leased as a nightlife destination ever since.[334]

The social highlight of 1985 was a February Valentine Benefit Ball, a glittering black-tie event featuring the crowning of a king and queen, and music provided by Albert Coleman's Orchestra. Proceeds from the affair benefited the Woman's Club Restoration Project and the Heart Association. Georgia governor Joe Frank Harris

Above, the view from the stage of the Atlanta Woman's Club auditorium (the Lucille King Thomas Auditorium), built in 1922. Below, the view of the stage. *Courtesy of the Kenan Research Center at the Atlanta History Center*

335 Atlanta Woman's Club Papers *1, Wimbish House Archives; Actor Cordell, "Woman's Club Restoration to Be Finished by this Fall," *The Atlanta Journal/The Atlanta Constitution Intown Extra*, 31 January 1985, Wimbish House Archives.

336 "Timeline 2010," Women's History and Resource Center, General Federation of Women's Clubs, Washington DC.

337 Darlene Rebecca Roth, *Matronage: Patterns in Women's Organizations, Atlanta, Georgia, 1890–1940* (Brooklyn: Carlson Publishing, 1994) 59–60.

338 Elliott, Beth, "Woman's Club Restoration Features Entertainment Complex," *Northside Neighbor*, Apr 1989, p.10, Wimbish House Archives; "Presidents' List," Wimbish House Archives.

honored the effort by declaring February 14 Atlanta Woman's Club Valentine Benefit Ball Day.[335]

On the national level, in 1984 the GFWC opened the Women's History and Resource Center to serve as a venue for research, workshops, lectures, and events that focused on the roles of volunteers and GFWC members in United States and women's history. The next year, GFWC International president Jeri Winger was chosen as an official US delegate to the United Nations "Decade for Women Conference" in Nairobi, Kenya. The event reinforced the Atlanta clubwomen's devotion to pursuing knowledge and experiences in international relations. The following year, clubwomen in Atlanta and throughout the country renewed their commitment to conservation, emphasizing preservation and the protection of endangered species.[336]

According to researcher and historian Darlene Roth, while social issues still took precedence, the role of the Atlanta Woman's Club was changing. Progress in areas of social welfare had placed the primary responsibility of tending to health and charitable endeavors in the hands of nonprofit organizations and government agencies. The Club's members, now less visible, were no longer in a position of having to manage and oversee these groups. Instead, they were forced into less prominent roles to help in procurement of funds, the push for legislation, and service.[337]

Presidents for the eighties were Mrs. Louise D. Rush (1980–1982), Mrs. Curtis H. Bryant (1982–1984), Mrs. Daisy Luckey Aukerman (1984–1986), Mrs. E. F. Rakestraw (1986–1988), Mrs. W. B. Zuber, (May 1988–February 1989), and Mrs. Daisy Luckey Aukerman (March 1989–May 1990).[338]

Mrs. Louise D. Rush
1980–1982

Mrs. Curtis H. Bryant
1982–1984

Mrs. Daisy Luckey Aukerman
1984–1986

Mrs. E. F. Rakestraw
1986–1988

Mrs. W. B. Zuber
May 1988–February1989

Mrs. Daisy Luckey Aukerman
March 1989–May 1990

CHAPTER TWENTY

The Atlanta Woman's Club's goals are to continue their productive participation in the Arts, Education, Conservation, Tallulah Falls School projects, Home Life, and International and Public Affairs, fostering the good and general welfare of the citizens in the immediate community, as well as the world-at-large through the advancement of civic and social improvement.

Mrs. Samuel (Lucy) Willard II[339]
Atlanta Woman's Club president, 1994–1996

he year 1990 was fraught with despair for the Atlanta Woman's Club. Burglars broke into the Wimbish House and stole irreplaceable antiques. To add to the misery, a month later thieves shattered a front window and stole the refrigerator. Then, on May 7, horrified members discovered that their headquarters had been gutted by a fire they suspected was caused by a short circuit in a freezer.[340] Raging through the clubhouse and decimating everything in its path, the flames almost completely destroyed the Wimbish House. At that time, the building housed both the Atlanta Woman's Club and the Petrus nightclub (later to become the Axys), which primarily suffered smoke and water damage.[341]

This was the first time the Club had been violated by burglary or fire, and members were shocked. According to former president Mildred Bryant, the ballroom suffered from smoke and water damage "but almost

339 "Willard Papers," Wimbish House Archives, Atlanta GA.

340 Mike Morris and Don Plummer, "Fire Hits City's 'Grand Old Lady,'" *Atlanta Journal*, Tuesday, 25 Sep 2001, Wimbish House Archives.

341 Cynthia Sapero, "Atlanta Woman's Club," papers, Wimbish House Archives; "Fire Guts Historic Mansion," *Atlanta Constitution*, 8 May 1990, Wimbish House Archives; Rebecca Rakoczy, "A Grand Old Lady Falls on Hard Times, Needs Help to Get a New Start," *Atlanta Journal Atlanta Constitution*, 3 February 1994, Wimbish House Archives.

342 Actor Cordell, "Woman's Club Determined to Make a Comeback After Fire," *Atlanta Constitution Intown Extra*, May 1990, Wimbish House Archives.

343 Ibid.

344 Mrs. Daniel H. (Louise) Vernon, "Notes," no date, courtesy Louise Vernon, Atlanta Woman's Club member.

345 Cordell, "Woman's Club Determined."

346 Vernon, "Notes," no date; Cordell, "Woman's Club Determined."

347 Louise Vernon, conversation with author Anne B. Jones, 15 December 2010.

348 In *Preservation Times* 10/2 (Summer 1990), Wimbish House Archives; Rakoczy, "A Grand Old Lady Falls On Hard Times." *Atlanta Journal Constitution* 3 February 1994. Wimbish House Archives.

349 Vernon, "Notes," no date; Letter from Architect Zachary W. Henderson to Louise Vernon, 4 Aug 1992, courtesy Louise Vernon; Rakoczy, "A Grand Old Lady Falls on Hard Times."

everything else was destroyed or badly damaged."[342] The Club had borrowed $250,000 for a renovation program that was almost complete, and the facility had been booked for months of community events. The fire destroyed the renovations and wiped out months of rental revenue. To make matters worse, the Club found its insurance coverage to be inadequate.[343]

At the time of the fire, two Club members, Mrs. Arnold Kent and Miss Lamar Sparks, were renting living quarters on the second floor. The House was also home to a variety of community groups that generally met on a monthly basis. These included the Atlanta Writers Club, the Business Women's Club, and others who suddenly found themselves uprooted.[344]

Many who observed the building's charred remains might have given up, but not the members of the Atlanta Woman's Club. Drawing upon the same energy they threw into social reform, the women immediately embarked on a financial campaign to save their home. "We are going to do everything possible to restore," said president Daisy Luckey Aukerman. "We are appealing to the public for funds. We feel we owe it to Atlanta not to lose this landmark. We think there should be a drive to restore it like the drive that saved the Fox Theatre."[345]

After the fire, city code inspectors stated that the facility could house no more tenants, so members decided to redecorate the second floor and designate it as one of the Club's events venues. The damaged antiques quickly underwent restoration and repair, and the women worked to recover records and memorabilia from the office. Fortunately, members were able to salvage the building's blueprints.[346]

Atlanta Woman's Club member Louise Vernon recalls the challenges of this strenuous time and the unfathomable amount of energy, donations, teamwork, and support Club members gave not only to the "Grand Old Lady," but also to each other. The conflagration "was both an emotional and financial blow to Club members," she stated.[347]

Commercial developers approached the Club with offers to purchase the property, but members gritted their teeth, fiercely determined to preserve their Atlanta treasure. As onlookers gazed upon the devastation, some spoke out, hoping their words would lend support. Noting that the house remained structurally sound, Atlanta's *Preservation Times* published encouraging words: "A rebuilt Wimbish House could offer space, not only for the Woman's Club, but also as a meeting or recreational facility for nearby corporations. The unique character of the Wimbish House could serve to enhance that section of Peachtree for all of its neighbors and for many admirers around the city."[348]

It was finally decided by members that restoration would be carried out by the Flagler Company under the watchful eyes of architect Zachary W. Henderson, who proclaimed the Wimbish House "a very grand example of our heritage." Henderson, who specializes in the restoration of older homes, took special interest in the project, welcoming the opportunity to help prevent the Wimbish House from being torn down to make way for "nondescript modern structures."[349]

During the first years after the fire, members met at a variety of sites to continue their active support and involvement in the Georgia and General Federations. In 1994, the Club began meeting at the Peachtree Presbyterian Church. The women held fast to tradition and each other, treating new members to orientation brunches at the Capital City Brookhaven Country Club and pushing forward despite their massive setback.[350]

Undaunted by the project's lengthy lack of completion, on 13 November 1995, under the leadership of club president Mrs. Samuel L. (Lucy) Willard, the Atlanta Woman's Club convened for its 100th Anniversary at Peachtree Presbyterian Church with a "When You Were Sweet Sixteen" celebration and a theme of "Music and Memories." The Arts Department contributed to the Student Art Fund and presented a professional organ concert featuring music from 1895 into the 1940s. Each member was presented with a Special Award of Appreciation 100th Anniversary certificate.[351] "For a century, the Atlanta Woman's Club members have exhibited vision, leadership, and positive community action."[352] Such were the accolades Atlanta newspapers offered in tribute to the occasion.[353]

During this time, the Club focused its efforts on maintaining and increasing membership, which had declined due to the fire and the inconvenience it caused. The Club also continued its humanitarian works and its expanding involvement in Tallulah Falls School. Members struggled to keep the Club afloat and well-connected to the Georgia Federation, the General Federation, and other clubs. The women attended state conventions, district meetings, and Tallulah Falls School events. President Lucy Willard toured the GFWC Headquarters in Washington, DC, and visited Federation Club meetings in Maryland and Arizona. She was so affected by the need for funding for the headquarters facilities that she later became chairman of Georgia's 1734 Society, repeatedly collecting statewide contributions totaling more than any other state in the nation.

Despite the challenges, the Club moved forward. Likewise, Tallulah Falls School broke ground for two new structures, the Federation Dining Hall and the Lettie Pate Evans Student Center.[354] "The Atlanta Woman's Club has an impressive history of contributions, socially and culturally," said Mrs. Willard in her 1994–1996 club yearbook, "to the city, the state, reaching beyond its borders, improving the lives of many in hospitals, women's prisons, schools, and missions. Through community involvement and legislative activities, the Club continues an ever-expanding role as a valuable asset for all." With changing times and conditions an ever-present challenge, the Club struggled to maintain its place in the National and State Federations' Arts, Conservation, Education, Home Life, International Affairs and Public Affairs Departments under the circumstances of the fire. As always there remained ever-present pleas to assist with unforeseen humanitarian needs.[355]

Continuing its activities and social services, the Club remained dedicated to making life better for all people, including prisoners, students, teachers, children, the elderly, and victims of natural disasters. Members concerned themselves with legislative and community issues, continued to enhance Atlanta's beauty by planting trees, and participated in projects for CARE, recycling and environmental awareness, scholarship programs, Canine Companions for Independence, the GaFWC Healthier Babies Campaign, and St. Jude's Ranch for Children. Major fundraisers included cookbook sales and a "No Bake" sale to help provide for donations.[356]

350 No author, "The Atlanta Woman's Club—A Brief History: 1994–1996," Wimbish House Archives.

351 Mrs. Samuel L. (Lucy) Willard, Atlanta Woman's Club Yearbook, 1994–1996, Wimbish House Archives.

352 "The Atlanta Woman's Club Celebrates 100 Years," *Northside Neighbor*, 8 Nov 1995, Wimbish House Archives.

353 Lucy Willard, "The Atlanta Woman's Club: A Brief History of My Term as President from 1994–1996," Wimbish House Archives.

354 "Celebrating 100 Years of Excellence," *Tallulah Falls School Magazine* 30/3 (Fall 2008): 32.

355 Lucy Willard, Atlanta Woman's Club Yearbook, 1994–1996.

356 Lucy Willard, The Atlanta Woman's Club—A Brief History: 1994–1996.

357 Morris and Plummer, "Fire Hits City's 'Grand Old Lady.'"

358 Zachary Henderson, interviews with Anne B. Jones, 1 Nov 2010, 16 Nov 2010.

359 Lucy Willard, The Atlanta Woman's Club—A Brief History: 1994–1996.

360 Lucy Willard, The Atlanta Woman's Club: Brief History, Fifth District GaFWC, 1995–1996, Wimbish House Archives.

Years passed before the Wimbish House was fully restored. At an estimated cost of two million dollars, insurance payouts combined with members' and others' contributions funded the rebuilding project. Architect Zachary Henderson helped in the building's return to glory. His Roswell firm researched related historical records and was integral in restoring the mansion to its original beauty.[357]

Today, "Zac," as he prefers to be called, still remembers walking past the house as a child. An orphan, he was raised by his widowed Aunt Claudine Wimbish, who lived nearby. The coincidence of names and possible relationship to the original owners spurred his interest in the project, as did the opportunity to save the precious landmark.

The Wimbish House included all the elements of a good project. It was a beautiful old house with a clientele who understood its significance and the significance of restoring it authentically. You couldn't walk past that property without feeling the presence of the grand Southern women who had come before. Their spirits touched me as I pondered what had been and what could be. I wanted to keep the spirit of those women in the building. I have a love for the Wimbish House and its history. It couldn't help but be a special project. The most difficult part was finding the money to do the project correctly with the same appearance. Some of the stones had become so hot, they were burned and destroyed. We had to devise ways to work with limited dollars.[358]

The historical research was a labor of love. After the Club was restored, Zac's wife Lynne, an artist, created a painting depicting the Wimbish House restoration. The Hendersons donated a print for the Club's 2010 Holiday Party silent auction.

On 13 January 1996, the year Atlanta hosted the Olympics, members convened for a general meeting in the Wimbish House's renovated clubroom, even though the overall renovation was not complete. New and refinished furniture and other items were installed to restore the home's elegance, not only for members' enjoyment, but also to maximize the building's potential as an events venue; rental revenue was necessary for the Club's survival. The main priority of the Club was to "restore the damaged clubhouse, bring it up to state-of-the-art standards for future successes," and make sure it continued to meet building safety codes.[359]

In April 1996, the Club invited State and District officers, members of sister clubs, and other visitors to an elaborate tea held in the ballroom against a backdrop of piano and violin music. Guests enjoyed refreshments and a tour of the clubhouse. That same year, First Night Atlanta held a family-oriented celebration in the Club House Ballroom.[360]

Looking back on that difficult time, later club president Cynthia Sapero remarked:

The easy thing to do would have been to give up and allow a wrecking crew to wipe away every trace of heritage we have shared with the city. But, our leaders have never been that easily shaken. So, with an enormous amount of time, research and preservation, the Wimbish House was restored to its original beauty, with some modern additions, such as an elevator and access ramps. The home is again enjoyed by our members and parties celebrating special occasions in the clubhouse, or by those who just pause to gaze inquisitively for a moment from the sidewalk outside the iron fencing.[361]

In 1999, the Atlanta Woman's Club sponsored Youth Art Week, which Atlanta's mayor Bill Campbell formally proclaimed. Members actively participated by sharing students' artwork and contributing to the Creating Pride Organization. Clubwomen also worked to support the Callanwolde Fine Arts Center and the Atlanta Symphony Orchestra's annual Decorators' Show House, as they continue to do year after year.[362]

Other important projects of this period included work related to the Atlanta Day Shelter for Women and Children, the Atlanta police Teddy Bear Drive, women's health awareness, recycling, conservation, education, and progress at Tallulah Falls School. Members marked a major accomplishment by establishing a library for students in Gwinnett County's juvenile detention center. Major fundraisers included a "Marty Gras" party in honor of Mart Dekom, president of the Atlanta Jaycees, and a "Queen Victoria's Birthday Party" cosponsored by the Victorian Society. Monies raised were used for clubhouse repair and maintenance. Members volunteered at numerous charity functions and sites, including a local VA hospital.[363]

Mrs. T. W. Marshall
May 1990-December 1991

In 1994, Atlanta Woman's Club members rejoiced as the renovated Atlanta Municipal Market became the Sweet Auburn Curb Market and regained its recognition as an "in" spot among those hungry for fresh country food. In 1999, the market gained national recognition and celebrity status when President Bill Clinton stopped by for sweet potato cheesecake.[364]

While in recovery from their devastating fire, Atlanta Woman's Club members witnessed with pride the United States Secretary of the Interior designate GFWC headquarters a National Historic Landmark. Three years later, GFWC founder Jane Cunningham Croly was inducted into the National Women's Hall of Fame in Seneca Falls, New York.[365]

During these trying years, the Atlanta Woman's Club was led by Mrs. T. W. Marshall (May 1990–December 1991), Mrs. Robert B. Vance, Sr. (January 1992–May 1994), Mrs. Samuel L. Willard, II (1994–1996), Mrs. Clyde A. Turner (1996–1998), and Dr. Sarah Helen Killgore (1998–2000). With the re-gentrification of Atlanta's Midtown, the Atlanta Woman's Club developed a stronger community presence symbolizing rootedness and stability. Along with

Mrs. Robert B. Vance, Sr.
January 1992-May 1994

361 Sapero, "Atlanta Woman's Club: Our History," Wimbish House Archives.

362 Atlanta Woman's Club Yearbook: 1998–2000, pp. 11–12, Wimbish House Archives.

363 Atlanta Woman's Club Yearbook: 1998–2000, pp. 12–15; Sapero, President's Report 2000, Wimbish House Archives.

364 Milo Ippolito, "Curb Market Milestone," *Atlanta-Journal Constitution*, October 2003, Wimbish House Archives; "80-Plus Years of Market for Sweet Auburn," *Atlanta Journal*, Wimbish House Archives.

365 Consisting in Timeline Calendar 2010, Women's History and Resource Center, General Federation of Women's Clubs, Washington DC.

366 "Notes," Wimbish House Archives.

other activities, members continued to enjoy club events such as luncheons, programs, and bridge.[366]

Mrs. Samuel L. Willard, II
1994–1996

Mrs. Clyde A. Turner
1996–1998

Mrs. Sarah Helen Killgore
1998–2000

CHAPTER TWENTY-ONE

The most important thing I have learned from being a member of the Atlanta Woman's Club is how a diversity of membership and a diversity of ideas and beliefs can be brought together in a capable, peaceful way. We're not quitters. We address almost all aspects of life, family, culture, health, schools, education, the arts, and do fun things that make us well-rounded.

Dr. Sarah Helen Killgore[367]
Atlanta Woman's Club president, 1998–2000

he Atlanta Woman's Club members entered the new millennium focused on doing good deeds for their community. Members have actively engaged in relationships with the Rainbow House, the Ronald McDonald House, the Samaritan House, DARE, CARE, the Veteran's Hospital, and nursing homes. Among their contributions have been donations of food, clothing, and monies for needy local organizations such as battered women's shelters. Members have purchased books and magazines for female prisoners and supported the Canine Companions program. They have volunteered funds, time, and effort for other endeavors such as recycling and environmental awareness programs, the Campaign for Healthier Babies, the Tour of Homes, the Callanwolde Fine Arts Center, and breast cancer detection and prevention.[368]

Beginning in 2000, the Club has been a member of Midtown Alliance, an organization devoted to initiatives supporting the revitalization and progress of Atlanta's Midtown area. Members have remained heavily

---

[367] Transcript, Dr. Sarah Helen Killgore's interview with Tom Thomson, summer 2009, Wimbish House Archives.

[368] Letter to Mr. Lee Morris, city council member, from Atlanta Woman's Club Board of Trustees member Elizabeth M. Burris, 4 Feb 2000, Wimbish House Archives.

369 Letter to Mr. Lee Morris from Elizabeth M. Burris, 4 Feb 2000; "Midtown Alliance: Share The Vision," www.midtownalliance.org/MA_over view.html

370 Sapero, "Atlanta Woman's Club: Our History." Wimbish House Archives.

371 Ibid.

372 Ibid.

373 Morris and Plummer, "Fire Hits City's 'Grand Old Lady,'" *Atlanta Journal*, Tues, 25 Sep 2001, Wimbish House Archives; Letter to Mr. Joseph Smith from Atlanta Woman's Club president Liz Burris, 18 Mar 2002, Wimbish House Archives.

involved in their traditional roles of support for education, literacy, and the arts, and they enjoy numerous programs related to social issues, music, literature, art, and wellness.[369]

As Atlanta has undergone changes, the Club has continued to work and "actively participate in making a difference."[370] According to Cynthia Sapero, AWC president 2000–2002, members continued to lead projects in a variety of areas, such as "beautifying Grady Hospital's student quarters, serving on the advisory committee of the Better Business Bureau, and establishing numerous scholarship programs." Other projects include contributing time and financial assistance "to the River Keepers to clean our rivers and streams and to the Veterans Administration to support our veterans."[371]

The Atlanta Woman's Club continues to support the city's arts, such as through its alliance with the Atlanta Symphony Orchestra; work with the Make-A-Wish Foundation, "an organization dedicated to terminally ill children"; and contributions to Operation Smile, "a group of medical personnel treating children in third-world countries that need corrective surgery for cleft palate conditions." Clubwomen have met with elected officials to "lobby for laws to improve the quality of life for all citizens, such as crime prevention, safety on our highways, and education." As a member of both the Chamber of Commerce and the Visitors Bureau, the Club has imparted to these groups a unique perspective.[372]

On Tuesday, 5 September 2001, the Atlanta Woman's Club Wimbish House headquarters was again heavily damaged by fire that began in the basement. According to *Atlanta Journal* reports, the blaze moved up through the second floor before breaking through the roof around an elevator shaft. The three-alarm fire was reported at approximately 6:30 A.M. No one was inside the building and there were no injuries, although more than fifty firefighters battled the blaze into late morning. The cause of the fire was undetermined. Ironically, the building had recently passed its fire inspection, which included the electrical systems.[373]

According to then-president Liz Burris, "The tragedy came on the heels of years of work on the part

Mrs. Cynthia Sapero, Sr.
May 2000–March 2002

Mrs. Elizabeth Burris
2002–2004

Mrs. Daisy Luckey Aukerman
2004–2006

Mrs. Susan Sumner Carter
2006–2008

Mrs. Karen M. Thomson
2008–2010

Mrs. Karen Bacheller
2010–2012

of the Atlanta Woman's Club members to renovate the facility."[374] Again, the women set about repairing the Wimbish House, never doubting that their place in the city would survive—and survive it has, for over a hundred years. So esteemed is the organization and its facilities that Georgia Public Television featured the Club on its documentary "Peachtree Street—Take Another Look."[375]

Despite what the club members experienced in the early part of the millennium, their support for Tallulah Falls School was business as usual. One of the Club's projects in 2005 involved working with the Georgia Federation in completely renovating Lipscomb Cottage, one of the original campus buildings. Beautifully decorated, the house is now the home office of the Georgia Federation of Women's Clubs. In 2008, the GaFWC opened a fifty-five-room lodge across from the school's main gate, which in 2011 was incorporated into the school's facilities, becoming a thriving middle school. The Lucy A. Willard Middle School was named for the AWC former president. Tallulah Falls School celebrated its centennial with yearlong celebrations, performances, and festivities. The Atlanta Woman's Club is currently in the process of renovating the old Trustees' Cottage to make it suitable for modern-day use.[376]

Presidents of the new millennium have included Mrs. Cynthia (Philip) H. Sapero, Sr. (May 2000–March 2002), Mrs. Elizabeth Burris (April 2002–June 2004), Mrs. Daisy Luckey Aukerman (2004–2006), Mrs. Susan (Larry) Carter (2006–2008), Dr. Karen (Tom) Moore Thomson (2008–2010), and Mrs. Karen (John) Bacheller (2010–2012).[377]

The Sweet Auburn Curb Market, originally the Municipal Market, is still going strong, now enhanced with a wide diversity of international products and faces. Called a "melting pot" because it appeals to people of all tastes and nationalities, its offerings range from Southern classics, such as chitterlings, to tofu. The market celebrates "Georgia Grown" but encourages unusual culinary delights and multicultural events.[378]

On the national level, in 2004 General Federation members contributed $180,000 to purchase a fully-equipped ambulance for the New York City Fire

374 Letter to Smith from Burris.

375 "Welcome to the Atlanta Woman's Club," flyer, no date, Wimbish House Archives.

376 *Tallulah Falls School Magazine* 30/3 (Fall 2008): 33–34, in Wimbish House Archives.

377 "Presidents' List," Wimbish House Archives.

378 Jon Waterhouse, "*At 80, Market Still Multi-Flavored Fun,*" AJC *accessAtlanta*, Oct 2003.

379 "Timeline 2010," Women's History and Resource Center, General Federation of Women's Clubs, Washington DC.

Department, replacing equipment lost during the September 11, 2001, terrorist attacks. Four years later, the GFWC successfully advocated for the Lilly Ledbetter Fair Pay Act, which was signed into law in January 2009. That same year, GFWC celebrated the twenty-fifth anniversary of the Women's History and Resource Center with new exhibits and an online catalog showcasing GFWC collections.[379]

CHAPTER TWENTY-TWO

The Atlanta Woman's Club is unique. I give my time to help build a future worthy of the sacrifice of women who had great vision, women who gave their best. I'm glad to be a part of it.

Daisy Luckey Aukerman[380]
Three-term Atlanta Woman's Club president

In a 2009 interview, Daisy Luckey Aukerman stated, "The Atlanta Woman's Club is a nonprofit philanthropic organization made up of professional women of all ages, races, and religions who share a common goal: to work together to improve our local community, socially, physically, culturally, and educationally. The Club is an active part of the General Federation of Women's Clubs (an international philanthropic organization headquartered in Washington, DC) and the Georgia Federation of Women's Clubs." The General Federation of Women's Clubs is the oldest and largest non-denominational, non-partisan international service organization of volunteer women with an outreach of thousands throughout the world. The Atlanta Woman's Club remains an active member of GFWC and GaFWC. For over a century, the Atlanta Woman's Club has been involved in community and national needs, including promoting the quality of life in the city of Atlanta, education, preserving natural resources, stressing good citizenship, encouraging healthy lifestyles, contributing to world peace and international understanding, and supporting participation in the arts.[381]

The Atlanta Woman's Club serves as a springboard for the development of individual potential and talents, offering role models, mentors, and leadership. In this modern time, members are life-coaches for each other

380 Transcript, Daisy Luckey Aukerman interview with Dr. Tom Thomson, summer 2009, Wimbish House Archives.

381 "Welcome to the Atlanta Woman's Club," paper, no date, Wimbish House Archives.

382 "General Federation of Women's Clubs Newsletter," 12 Mar 2010.

383 Ibid., 7 Mar 2010.

384 Letter to Mr. Lee Morris, city council member, from Atlanta Woman's Club board of trustees member Elizabeth M. Burris, 4 Feb 2000, Wimbish House Archives.

385 Atlanta Woman's Club Papers #1, Wimbish House Archives; Sapero, "Atlanta Woman's Club," paper, May 2000–March 2002, Wimbish House Archives; "Experience the Crown Jewel of Midtown," flyer, no date, Wimbish House Archives.

386 "The Atlanta Woman's Club Celebrates 100 Years," *Northside Neighbor*, 8 Nov 1995, Wimbish House Archives.

and those they serve, offering enlightenment and friendship, truly living the Club's motto, "More Light."

The Club's work is ongoing, especially in the areas of Literacy Action, the Georgia Justice Project, Domestic Violence Awareness, aid for the disabled, support for the arts and education, conservation, international affairs, and contributions for Tallulah Falls School. Following the General Federation of Women's Clubs' emphasis on assistance for victims of the Haiti earthquake, the Atlanta Woman's Club presented an informational program and gave donations in connection with Habitat for Humanity and the Haitian relief effort.[382]

Under guidance from the General Federation's Women's Resource Center, members have begun videotaping and recording oral histories, which are meticulously transcribed and stored for future generations. Entering the technological world of social media, AWC members have joined sister clubs and the GFWC in establishing internet web sites and chat sites and an international online book club.[383]

Leading the preservation of this dynamic club and its unparalleled headquarters is an enthusiastic group of ladies determined to unite their diversity of talents and experiences into a force for the good of their community and the growth and development of their fellow members. Making full use of income received from facility rental fees, membership dues, and donations, these devoted women continue to aid those in need; address local, national, and global issues; give time and support to Tallulah Falls School; and maintain the historic Wimbish House, one of the state's most beautiful examples of turn-of-the-century architecture.[384]

One of the few remaining Peachtree Street mansions, the Wimbish House retains pieces of its original furnishings, pictures dating back to the 1800s, and lavish interior detail. Due to its uniqueness and beauty, this marvelous clubhouse remains the site of elegant community gatherings and is occasionally used as a movie set. The Wimbish House and its grounds continue to serve as a venue for Atlanta Woman's Club meetings and major Atlanta events, including weddings, receptions, parties, corporate events, teas, and other upscale affairs. Atlantans refer to the Club's expansive facilities as the "Crown Jewel of Midtown."[385]

Celebrity guests have included first ladies, screen stars, actresses, opera stars, and notables from all areas of the arts. For well over 100 years, "the Atlanta Woman's Club members have exhibited vision, leadership, and positive community action."[386]

An excerpt from the late Cynthia Sapero's paper entitled "Atlanta Woman's Club" aptly expresses the history and goals of this remarkable membership:

We still have teas served with silver, crystal, and china, with some women wearing hats and dressing up just for the fun of it. But, our members are leaders in the fields of art, business, the legal and medical fields, and the political arena. Our voices are still heard at City Hall and the Capitol; and most corporate executives take notice when we approach them for their support on community relations issues. The words used to describe our purpose were beautifully stated by the former president of the Georgia Federation of Women's Clubs, Mrs. Jerry Peters, . . . "I have often been asked about a woman's place in this changing world. As a young woman I remember resenting the expression 'woman's place.' I never heard anyone speak of a man's place. It really is very simple. Woman's place is everywhere. It is where schools are not adequate, where communities need improvement, where government needs support and legislation demands action. Women are needed where children live and grow and develop into responsible adults. Woman's place is everywhere, as long as she has eyes to see and appreciate, ears to hear and understand, and a soul that yearns, a soul that knows when something is not right."

And so it goes, for more than a century, the Atlanta Woman's Club's members have brought happiness, beauty and fulfillment to many people, and it is with an invincible spirit we continue on.

As the city changes, the Club continues to participate actively in making a difference. A world of opportunity awaits members of the network of women volunteering on local, state and national levels. You can find that satisfaction that comes from making a difference in the community, experiencing the support of women with mutual concerns and interests, and the exchange of ideas.[387]

A force for the good of Atlanta, their state and the world, the Atlanta Woman's Club is poised to continue its positive leadership. "With the continued support of interested groups and additional members," the Club looks forward to having an even larger impact in the years to come.[388]

According to former president Liz Burris, members of the Atlanta Woman's Club have the opportunity to network with government, corporate, and organizational leaders and to influence public opinion while developing and using leadership skills and personal talents. "There is a broad choice of programs from which you may gain international contacts, as well as new acquaintances within our strong national network."[389]

Most important, and in conclusion, are these words from the 1972 President's Report by Mrs. Edward O. Snow: "Through the years no worthy cause has knocked at her door and not found a ready response and help. Many reforms were brought about in city affairs, the prisons, schools, libraries, hospitals, etc. The members of the Atlanta Woman's Club have been back of every great movement for social, humanitarian, and cultural improvement."[390]

387 Excerpt from Sapero, "Atlanta Woman's Club," Wimbish House Archives.

388 "The Atlanta Woman's Club Celebrates 100 Years," Northside Neighbor, 8 Nov. 1995, Wimbish House Archives.

389 Liz Burris, "Letter to New Members," no date, Wimbish House Archives.

390 "Down Memory Path," in President's Report, 1970–1972, Wimbish House Archives.

EPILOGUE

by Rose Ditto

or over 100 years the Atlanta Woman's Club has fulfilled the Club's objectives, which were established from its very beginning in 1895, exemplifying those of their parent organization, the General Federation of Women's Clubs, founded in 1890. The AWC's three-fold objectives have been social, literary, and humanitarian-worthy efforts for their members and for their community, and continue to be so. The Club continues to work toward these ends today.

One possibly wonders how an organization lasts for over 100 years and continues to thrive. Admittedly, many clubs throughout our nation have not survived as the GFWC Atlanta Woman's Club has, but some have. Even though the GFWC membership was larger many years ago, we still have over 100,000 members and can claim that we are the oldest and the largest women's volunteer organization.

GFWC's survival comes from the wisdom of our founders and our early leaders. The organization is "general," which includes fitting "all things in life" into the organization's framework. It is nonpartisan and non-faith-based, which means it is inclusive of all women, no matter their race, religion, or beliefs. "Unity in Diversity" was wisely selected as our motto portraying power! Our purpose is that of working together for the common good, making a difference in our communities, in our nation, and in our world. Our mission statement has become "The General Federation of Women's Clubs is an international women's organization dedicated to community improvement by enhancing the lives of others through volunteer service."

When we as human beings focus on giving of ourselves and enhancing the lives of others, we also enhance our own lives. Self-worth comes from within, and it develops through knowing we are valued and have a purpose for living. There is a need in our nation and in our world for improvement of people's self-worth. We witness too much violence, abuses of drugs and alcohol, and many other negative behaviors.

There is a strong need for GFWC to prosper, to thrive. We must mentor our young people to understand the value of volunteering. We must build new GFWC clubs and reach younger members. Our communities, our nation, and our world will benefit as they have for over 100 years. Yes, we can do it—we must!

—Rose Ditto, Ph.D.
International GFWC President, 2008–2010

A FINAL WORD

by Karen Bacheller

nd so we continue, each of us feeling and hoping that what we do for our organization will serve the community and allow the Atlanta Woman's Club to grow and prosper. Mindful that our enduring mission is to better the lives of those in our world and community, we ask the question: "What is needed?"

—Karen Bacheller
Atlanta Woman's Club President, 2010–2012

ABOUT THE ATLANTA WOMAN'S CLUB TODAY

by Karen M. Thomson

ffiliated with the international General Federation of Women's Clubs (GFWC), the Atlanta Woman's Club supports the GFWC motto "Unity in Diversity." The AWC is a diverse group of women working together toward a common purpose. We are nonprofit, nonpartisan, and nonsectarian, and any woman in agreement with our purpose is welcome to become a member. Clearly our mission is, and has always been, to better the lives of people in our community and in our world through volunteer and philanthropic service. Our founding president, Rebecca Douglas Lowe, described our purpose as being three-fold: "literary, social, and humanitarian."

We refer to the various humanitarian endeavors—i.e., our Club work—as our "Federation work," our *raison d'etre.* Guided by the GFWC and the Georgia Federation of Women's Clubs (GaFWC), the Atlanta Woman's Club has six focal areas, now called Community Service Programs: Arts, Conservation, Education, Home Life, International Outreach, and Public Issues. Though not considered a Community Service Program, Tallulah Falls School is another focal point of AWC support. Each member chooses where she would like to serve. The Atlanta Woman's Club is currently a part of GaFWC's Fifth District. We value our role as an active member and participant in district, state, regional, national, and international meetings and conventions.

Our business meetings are luncheons held on the second Monday of each month, September through June, 11:00 AM–1:00 PM. Luncheon reservations are required.

For more information on the Atlanta Woman's Club and the Wimbish House, please visit our websites: atlwc.org and thewimbishhouse.com.

—Karen M. Thomson, Ph.D.
Atlanta Woman's Club President, 2008–2010
Director, AWC History Book Project
Chair, History Book Committee, 2008-2012

Anne B. Jones, Ph.D., is the author of *Tides of Fear*, a thriller set on St. Simons Island; *STOP*, a manual for youth violence prevention; *Gold Thunder*, an autobiography of 1960 NASCAR champion Rex White; *All Around the Track*, a collection of racing mini-memoirs; and *Brave at Heart*, the story of photographer Walter Victor and the Atlanta Braves. *STOP* was published and released by the Atlanta Council on Battered Women, distributed nationwide, and included as part of the television documentary *Behind Closed Doors*. Dr. Jones was nominated for Georgia Author of the Year for *Brave at Heart* in 2007 and for *Tides of Fear* in 2012.

Having specialized in working with at-risk students for thirty-one years, Dr. Jones taught in a variety of school settings, including Job Corps, Boys and Girls Town (a shelter for status offenders), and DeKalb Alternative School (an educational center for suspended students). She has been a volunteer mediator, rape crisis counselor, victim-witness assistant, volunteer probation officer, public relations writer, and member of the Gwinnett County Domestic Violence Task Force.

Dr. Jones has published hundreds of feature articles on topics ranging from crime prevention to personality profiles and makes frequent presentations on writing and publishing topics at bookstores, civic organizations, and writing workshops. She is a member of the Atlanta Woman's Club.

Dr. Jones may be contacted via e-mail at annebjones@msn.com or on her website: www.annebjones.com.

 Aryc W. Mosher's twenty-plus years in international health efforts have provided him with a wonderful backdrop to enjoy his hobby-cum-career of photography. For Aryc, photography carves out small slivers of the world for others to notice and to celebrate. The knot in an old door, the light through a child's hair, the curve of a drying leaf each becomes a world of its own. This is the vantage point from which Aryc aims his lens. His vision has produced fascinating images that capture emotion and enhance the beauty of his subjects. His unique images are able to create moments that can support the work of international organizations or enhance personal moments of people celebrating life.

It is through his working in international health with the Carter Center that Aryc became acquainted with the Atlanta Woman's Club's goal to write a book celebrating its history and contributions to the greater Atlanta community. He immediately volunteered his skill in photo restoration and portrait photography.

To put it in Aryc's words, "This has been a wonderful collaboration! The women of the Atlanta Woman's Club are an amazing group of warm-hearted and charming professional women and truly are a treasure to Atlanta and the state of Georgia."

Aryc can be contacted through his photography studio, M-Square Photography, or its web site: www.msquarephoto.com.

BIBLIOGRAPHY

The author and the AWC Book Committee utilized dozens of newspaper clippings, typed notes, scrapbooks, interview transcripts, and other files found in the Wimbish House Archives in Atlanta, Georgia; at the Kenan Research Center of the Atlanta History Center in Atlanta, Georgia; and in the personal collection of Daisy Luckey Aukerman. While not included here, those sources are listed in the footnotes of the book. For more information about the Atlanta Woman's Club—both current and past—see the club website at www.atlwc.org.

BOOKS

Ambrose, Andy. *Atlanta: An Illustrated History*. Athens GA: Hill Street Press, 2003. In Kenan Research Center, Atlanta History Center.

Blass, Kimberly S., and Michael Rose. *Atlanta Scenes: Photojournalism in the Atlanta History Center Collection*. Charleston SC: Arcadia, 2003.

Cooper, Walter Gerald. *Official History of Fulton County*. Atlanta: Walter W. Brown Publishing Co., 1934.

Garrett, Franklin M. *Atlanta and Environs: A Chronicle of Its People and Events*. Volumes 1 and 2. New York: Lewis Historical Pub. Co., 1987.

Hancock, Carol Stevens. *Not by Magic, But by Faith, Courage, and Earnest Work*. Toccoa GA: Commercial Printing Company, 1982.

———. *The Light in the Mountains: A History of Tallulah Falls School*. Toccoa GA: Commercial Printing Company, 1975, 1990.

Harlan, Louis E., Raymond W. Smock, Barbara S. Kraft. *The Booker T. Washington Papers*. Volume 5: 1899–1900. Chicago: University of Illinois Press, 1976.

Houde, Mary Jean. *Reaching Out: A Story of the General Federation of Women's Clubs*. Chicago: Mobium Press, 1989.

McCuller, Bernice. *This Is Your Georgia*. Montgomery AL: Viewpoint Publications, Inc., 1972.

Roth, Darlene R., and Louise E. Shaw. "From Center Stage to Center Court." In *Atlanta Women from Myth to Modern Times: A Century of History*. Atlanta: Atlanta Historical Society, 1980.

Roth, Darlene R. *Matronage: Patterns In Women's Organizations, Atlanta, Georgia, 1890–1940*. Brooklyn NY: Carlson Publishing Company, 1994.

Staman, A. Louise. *Loosening Corsets*. Macon GA: Tiger Iron Press, 2006.

Wells, Mildred White. *Unity in Diversity*. Volume 2. Washington, DC: General Federation of Women's Clubs, 1975.

ARTICLES AND WEBSITES

Biehl, Ada. "Woman's Club Celebrates 75th Year Serving City." *Atlanta Journal-Constitution*. 1 November 1970.

"Celebrating 100 Years of Tallulah Falls School." *Tallulah Falls School Magazine* 30/3 (Fall 2008): 14–19.

Coles, Mrs. A. P. (Atlanta Woman's Club President). "Atlanta City Federation of Woman's Clubs." *Atlanta Constitution*, 4 June 1913.

"GaFWC History." *GFWC/Georgia Federation of Women's Clubs* website. www.gafwc.org/html/gafwc_history.html.

Hadin, Mrs. Charles J. (President of the Atlanta City Federation). "Atlanta City Federation of Woman's Clubs: Foreword." *Atlanta Constitution*. 4 June 1913.

"History." *Holy Innocents' Episcopal Church* website. www.holyinnocents.org/about/history.

"History." *Student Aid Foundation, Inc.* website. www.studentaidfoundation.org/history.html.

Johnson, Mrs. J. Lindsay. "Bills We've Lost and Won." *Atlanta Constitution*. 4 June 1913.

Mellawn, Muriel. "Lady Rhondda and the Changing Faces of British Feminism," *Frontiers: A Journal of Women's Studies* 9/2 (1987): 7–13.

"Mr. Jackson Voices Ideals of American Homes At Woman's Club." *Atlanta Journal*. 13 November 1923.

Newman, Harvey K. "Cotton Expositions in Atlanta." *History and Archaeology. The New Georgia Encyclopedia*. 25 October 2009. www.georgiaencyclopedia.org/ nge/Article.jsp?id=h-2913.

"Sweet Auburn Curb Market." *Project for Public Spaces* website. www.pps.org/great_public_spaces/one?public_place_id=182.

"Tech Glee Club to Present Opera *Martha*, May 2–3." *The Georgia Press*. 7 April 1945. Georgia Archives, ACC # 1975-0487M. Georgia Federation of Women's Clubs. Fifth District Records, unit 19.

"Twelfth Night To Be Celebrated." *Atlanta Constitution*. 10 January 1945. Georgia Archives, ACC# 1975-0487M. Georgia Federation of Women's Clubs. Fifth District Records, unit 19.

Welander, Suzanne. "Atlanta's Sweet Auburn Curb Market Carries On." *Edible Metro & Mountains* website. Fall 2009. www.ediblecommunities.com/metroandmountains/fall-2009/historic-urban-market.htm.

"Woman's Club to Meet, Hear Dr. Stubbs on 'Peace.'" *The Georgia Press-The North Side Press*. 10 February 1945. Georgia Archives, ACC # 1975-0487M. Georgia Federation of Women's Clubs. Fifth District Records, unit 19.

"Woman's Club to Present Three-Act Comedy on Jan. 19." *The Atlanta Constitution*. 8 January 1945. Georgia Archives, ACC # 1975-0487M. Georgia Federation of Women's Clubs. Fifth District Records, unit 19.

INDEX

Numbers in *italics* indicate images.